yo!
sushi

The Japanese Cookbook

Kimiko Barber

Collins

HarperCollins Publishers Ltd
77–85 Fulham Palace Road
London
W6 8JB

The Collins website address is: www.collins.co.uk

Collins is a registered trademark of HarperCollins Publishers Ltd.

First published in 2007

ISBN 978 0 00 724128 6

Food Photography: Frank Adam
Food styling: Jane Suthering
Editorial Director: Jenny Heller
Senior Editor: Lizzy Gray
Designers: Nicky Barneby and Emma Ewbank

Colour reproduction by Colourscan, Singapore
Printed in China

contents

foreword by Robin Rowland

Welcome to the YO! Sushi cookbook, which is a collection of some of our favourite dishes as well as a celebration of our tenth anniversary. We've chosen all our classics like salmon sashimi, maki and nigiri, and a great collection of hot favourites as well. With the help of our established and wonderful author Kimiko Barber, we've shown the experts' way of cutting and slicing fish and then of course how to roll sushi, which is something even I had to do at my first few weeks at YO! Sushi eight years ago! Kimiko has also introduced a selection of new additions to our menu especially for making at home.

When Simon Woodroffe launched YO! Sushi on Poland Street in Soho, London, in 1997 we were a brand new restaurant concept. Talking robots served drinks and karaoke played in the bar below. Today we have 40 restaurants in the UK and overseas, 1,000 staff and 3 million customers at our conveyor belts a year. We have a strong growth plan, but of course the food remains our core passion.

We also have no secrets at YO! Sushi – all the food is created by in-house chefs who prepare fresh food all day long using the highest-quality ingredients. The conveyor belt is the fashion show, providing real food theatre for the beautiful dishes.

In the restaurants we have colour-coded plates which have been reflected in this book throughout (green basics, blue sauces etc.)

to keep things simple and in the YO! Sushi style. Our customers tell us that the second they sit down at the belt they 'get it', which is an experience we have tried to reflect in this book.

On a final note, I'm personally really looking forward to being able to recreate my all time faves which are hairy prawns and coriander-seared tuna sashimi, so this book is going to be just as much fun for me and my family, as hopefully it will be for you. Thanks also to Mike Lewis, YO! Sushi's development chef, and Georgia Hall, head of marketing, who have worked closely with Kimiko and Collins to passionately make this book happen.

All that leaves me to say now is, ENJOY!

Robin Rowland (CEO)
YO! Sushi

YO! Sushi at home: an invitation to Japanese cooking

Some years ago I was fortunate enough to dine with a high-ranking Japanese official. As we traded views about world affairs, he suddenly confessed to me the secret of Japanese diplomacy. "This piece of sushi," he admitted somewhat ruefully, "has done more for Japan's reputation than all my official diplomatic efforts." He was perhaps too modest, I replied, but somehow I felt he had uttered a profound truth about the global influence of Japanese cuisine.

When I first came to England as a teen in the early 1970's, there were no more than a dozen Japanese restaurants in the entire country. Now there are more than a hundred in London alone, helped wildly by the popularity of YO! Sushi. In the ten years since the first YO! Sushi opened on Poland Street, Soho, there has been a Japanese food revolution. Today you'll find packs of sushi available next to sandwiches on supermarket shelves, there are takeaway sushi chains, I can order sushi deliveries direct to my door and my laptop no longer tries to spell-check 'sushi' into a girl's name. All this is beyond my wildest imaginings.

These days, I no longer have to make long treks to find the Japanese ingredients I grew up with – so many are now easily available in even remote towns and villages, and those that aren't I can order online. This is what

helps make the writing of *YO! Sushi The Japanese Cookbook* so exciting for me – I know that if I am asking you to find a certain ingredient, you're more than likely going to be able to source it fairly easily. I want to help demystify Japanese cooking at home, the way YO! Sushi has done for the restaurant diner.

To the uninitiated, Japanese food may seem intimidating or overly complicated to prepare. While it is true that some dishes require an attention to detail, there are so many dishes, including the sometimes mysterious sushi, that even the most inexperienced home cook can prepare. The main point to understand is that the basic principle of Japanese cuisine is to enhance, not to change what nature offers. This means that food is prepared and eaten, whenever possible, in its natural form. In Japan, we say 'less is more' and this applies to our ways of cooking.

The philosophy of Japanese cuisine is encapsulated by the 'five principles': five colours, five tastes, five ways of cooking, five senses and five attitudes. The first three cover the practical sides of cooking so that a meal is balanced and nutritious. The last two are more esoteric and philosophical.

- The five colours preach the virtue of having five coloured ingredients – white, red, yellow, green and black (which includes dark brown and purple), to provide a balanced and nutritious menu.

- The five tastes means a meal should combine a harmonious balance of saltiness, sourness, sweetness, bitterness and *umami* – the fifth sense of taste that was first formulated in 1908 by Kikunae Ikeda at the Tokyo Imperial University. Although there is no direct translation in English, *umami* describes a subtle savoury flavour which is found in many foods such as meat, fish, seaweeds, vegetables and cheeses.

- The third principle urges cooks to use five different cooking methods – boiling, grilling steaming, frying and combining flavours.

- The fourth deals with the sensual elements of food. Eating Japanese food engages all five senses, not just taste, which is in fact the last element after scent, vision, sound and feel.

- The final principle, five attitudes, is more spiritual and is based on Buddhist teachings: a man should respect and appreciate all human efforts and be grateful and humble of nature.

If all of this sounds too profound, you need not worry. Most young Japanese people today would be unable to recite, let alone explain, the big philosophical fives of our cuisine. What we do have is an innate, almost instinctive sense of composing a meal or choosing from a restaurant menu to eat a well-balanced harmonious meal – it is in our culture, it is in our blood!

So, how should you apply these principles in your own kitchen? The answer is to keep it simple. Choose the freshest and the best seasonal ingredients you can possibly buy from your local shops and markets and you are set for a winning start. Remember, the idea is not to change your ingredients but to bring out their best by doing less, not more. Let nature's offerings speak for themselves.

My aim for this book is to encourage you to take the fun and inclusive YO! Sushi dining experience into your home kitchen. The book is organised so that you can start with the basics and expand your repertoire from chapter to chapter as you gain experience. I invite you to join me in the pleasures of cooking Japanese food and to share it with your family and friends.

the basics

The secret to successful Japanese cooking is choosing the freshest ingredients, using traditional Japanese flavourings and mastering the basic techniques. This chapter includes basic recipes, such as dashi stock, explains ingredients that you may be unfamiliar with and shows through step-by-step pictures how to roll sushi, cut sashimi and make crispy tempura.

Many Japanese ingredients are now available in supermarkets or health food stores, and those that aren't can be found in Japanese stores or ordered online. See page 188 for a list of suppliers.

essential flavourings

There are five essential ingredients that are used either on their own or combined with each other to produce the distinctive Japanese tastes and flavours.

soy sauce (shoyu)

Soy sauce is probably the best known Japanese seasoning ingredient and is made from fermented soybeans, wheat, salt and water. Although there are many different types in Japan, there are three types that are available outside Japan. These are: dark, light and tamari. The dark all-purpose soy sauce is used for most of the recipes in this book unless specified otherwise. If you or anyone in your family suffers from wheat intolerance, use tamari, which should not contain wheat. However, as manufacturers often use the term loosely, always read the label carefully before buying. Slightly thicker and less salty than the other soy sauces, tamari is also used for dipping. Light soy sauce is much saltier than the dark variety and is used in cooking when dark soy sauce would discolour the food. Buy a small bottle of dark soy sauce if you prefer to keep only one type.

Available in glass or toughened plastic bottles, soy sauce is best kept tightly capped in a cool, dark kitchen cupboard or, better still, in the refrigerator, if you have room. Its subtle aroma does fade after several weeks so buy it in small quantities. You may find that small sodium crystals have begun to form around the cap during storage. These are not harmful – just wipe the bottle clean and continue to use it.

In response to recent concerns about daily salt intake, some reduced-sodium soy sauces are now available, but the flavour can be disappointing. If you want to reduce your salt intake choose recipes that require little or no salt, or dilute regular dark soy sauce with water or dashi (see pages 16–17). However, you will find that the recipes in this book use surprisingly little salt.

miso

Alongside soy sauce, miso is one of the most important seasonings in Japanese cooking and, like soy sauce, is made from fermented soybeans. It is an exceptionally healthy food, packed with vitamin E and minerals. During fermentation its soy protein is converted into an easily digestible form of amino acids. Miso lowers cholesterol and blood pressure, and is said to help ward off cancer.

Miso is available in different colours and textures, ranging from pale cream, called 'white', through to a light peanut butter and milk chocolate colour to a steely dark brown. The texture of different misos can also vary, from a soft cream cheese consistency to grainy, then dry and hard. In general, the darker the colour the harder and saltier the miso. A good all-purpose miso to use is a medium-brown, milk chocolate-coloured paste with a texture similar to cream cheese. You will probably find that you choose the most popular variety of rice miso, which is fermented by adding rice to cooked soybean mash. Others, however, are made from wheat, barley or soybeans alone.

Sold in plastic packaging or containers, miso is best transferred to an airtight container once opened. It will keep well for up to six months stored in the refrigerator.

vinegar

Every culinary culture has its own favourite vinegar and in Japan this is rice vinegar, which is a light golden colour with a mild and fragrant flavour. Throughout this book, use Japanese rice vinegar unless specified otherwise.

There are many brands of rice vinegar and each manufacturer produces several different grades. The grading of rice vinegar is quite similar to that of olive oil. *Junmai-su*, which means 'pure rice vinegar', is the highest quality – the equivalent of extra virgin olive oil – and is made from the first pressing of polished white Japanese rice. The next in order of quality and purity is *kome-su*, meaning 'rice vinegar'. Lower-quality vinegars contain added alcohol and are made from other grains. In general, price is a good indication of quality – buy the best quality you can afford for the finest flavour.

As vinegar darkens with age and through exposure to light, it should be stored in tightly capped glass bottles in a cool, dark kitchen cupboard. Its gentle aroma can begin to fade after the bottle has been open for several weeks, so it is best to buy a small quantity at a time and to use it as quickly as possible.

sake

Sake is Japan's traditional alcoholic drink and it has a long and intriguing history. It is distilled from steamed and fermented rice, is clear in appearance and has as many as 400 flavour components. Sake is assessed according to five basic qualities: dryness, sweetness, bitterness, acidity and astringency, or tartness. There are thousands of sake brewers across Japan and each manufacturer has its own unique combination of those five qualities. The brand of sake you choose is a matter of personal preference.

Although in recent years beer and wine have become the Japanese nation's favourite drinks, sake's cultural and culinary importance remains unchallenged. In the kitchen, sake performs many functions. It adds flavour and depth to dishes, is used as a cooking liquor and as a base for marinades and preserves, and to neutralise the strong smell of fish and meat. Table-quality dry sake is the most versatile – avoid 'cooking sake', which often has a strong artificial smell and is usually of an inferior grade that contains additives. Store sake tightly capped in a cool, dark kitchen cupboard and use within eight weeks of opening.

mirin

A sweet sake, mirin is used only for cooking. The best-quality mirin is made from rice in a process similar to that used for brewing sake. With a clear, amber-coloured, syrupy liquid and a faint aroma of sake, mirin is used as a sweetener and glazing agent to give food an attractive shine. Three teaspoons of mirin is the equivalent in sweetness of one teaspoon of sugar. Mirin has a relatively long shelf life, although its aroma fades soon after opening. It should be stored in a cool, dark kitchen cupboard until it is needed and stored in the refrigerator once opened. Use within eight weeks of opening.

basic ingredients – the YO! Sushi pantry

Listed below are basic ingredients that are used in many of the recipes in this book. Some of these may look strange and smell odd if you are not used to them, but they are easy to cook with and turn ordinary dishes into something special.

black and white sesame seeds Toasting sesame seeds gives them a rich flavour. You can buy them ready toasted, but if unavailable use raw sesame seeds, which are flatter in shape and lighter in colour, to toast yourself. Put them in dry frying pan over medium heat, and shake the pan frequently, for 5–7 minutes or until lightly toasted. Toasted sesame seeds will store for three months in a sealed container in a dark cupboard. If you are using them after one month it is best to re-toast them to revive their flavour.

bonito fish flakes The dried shavings or flakes of the bonito, or skipjack tuna, are used to flavour dashi stock (see pages 16–17). Traditionally, bonito fish flakes were sold in solid lumps to be shaved at home, but today, especially outside Japan, they are sold ready shaved. Do not buy too large a quantity at a time, as the distinctive smoky flavour fades quickly. Once opened, keep in an airtight bag and store in a dark, dry kitchen cupboard anduse within eight weeks.

dashinomoto This is an instant dashi stock powder that makes a useful stand-by for making dashi stock – the basic stock that is used in many Japanese recipes (see pages 16–17).

konbu (dried kelp seaweed) This dark green seaweed imparts a subtle flavour and is used for making dashi stock, the base for many Japanese dishes. Konbu grows up to 10m (33ft) long in the cold seas around the northern island of Hokkaido. It is sold dried, either ready-cut or in long strips. Once opened store in an airtight bag in a dark, dry kitchen cupboard and use within three months.

mushrooms You will find several varieties of Japanese mushrooms, especially shiitake (see below), used in the recipes for their individual qualities: shimeji for their distinct nutty flavour and aroma, enoki for their beautiful and delicate appearance and texture, and maitake for their lace-like appearance and fine taste. It has become increasingly easy to buy them fresh from supermarkets. **dried shiitake mushrooms** are used for their strong flavour. They first need to be reconstituted. Soak in warm water for 5–10 minutes then cut off and discard the stalks. The soaking liquid can be used in recipes to add richness.

noodles The noodles most frequently used in the recipes are: soba (thin, dark noodles made from buckwheat flour and therefore gluten-free), somen (a thin white noodle) and udon (a wheat-flour noodle that is thicker than the soba noodle). Other noodles include yakisoba noodles (soft semi-cooked Chinese-style egg noodles), sold in vacuum packs in supermarkets and often labelled 'stir-fry noodles', and harusame noodles (made from mung bean or potato starch).

nori This marine algae is formed into paper-like sheets and is an essential ingredient for making rolled sushi, such as maki rolls, hand rolls and inside-out rolls.

panko Also known as Japanese breadcrumbs, panko are coarse white breadcrumbs used to give a light and crunchy coating to fried food.

pickled sushi ginger is thinly sliced root ginger macerated in sweetened vinegar. It is served with sushi as a palate cleanser and digestive aid.

rice The short-grain Japanese rice, which supermarkets often sell as 'sushi rice', has a soft and sticky texture when cooked. (See pages 18–21 for instructions on how to cook rice and prepare sushi rice.)

sansho pepper This Japanese white pepper is made from the ground seedpods of the Japanese prickly ash and is used as a seasoning. It has a refreshing aroma of mint and basil with a touch of liquorice, similar to that of Sichuan pepper. It is often used with grilled oily fish and chicken.

shichimi togarashi Also known as Japanese seven-spice chilli powder, this seasoning is a blend of chilli, black and white sesame seeds, dried citrus peels and seaweeds. It is a traditional seasoning for noodles and yakitori.

tofu, or soybean curd, is a nutritious protein food made from soybeans. There are two main types: firm and silken. Firm tofu can be cut into slices or cubes, whereas silken tofu is a soft form of tofu rather like yogurt in consistency. Before using firm tofu, drain the liquid it has been stored in and rinse under cold running water. Then wrap it in kitchen paper and allow to stand for 15–20 minutes.

wakame This green, silky seaweed wakame is satin-like in texture and rich in vitamin A, calcium, minerals and fibre. A healthy food, it also lowers cholesterol and blood pressure. Wakame is often sold in dried form and once rehydrated is used in soups and salads.

wasabi is made from an aquatic plant that grows in Japan and has a distinct, strong flavour similar to horseradish. It is available in a powder or paste form. The powder form is more economical and keeps longer; to use, mix it with water until it forms a thick paste.

yuzu is a Japanese citrus fruit that looks like a yellow tangerine. It is used both for its peel and for its juice. Outside Japan the juice is sold in bottles. The juice is relatively expensive, as it comes from a very slow-growing plant. Once opened, yuzu juice should be stored in the refrigerator and used within eight weeks.

basic techniques

This section covers the basic techniques used in Japanese cooking. Preparing dashi stock and sushi rice are quick and easy to learn, and are the building blocks which will enable you to make countless dishes. Cutting sashimi as well as rolling and forming various kinds of sushi take time and practice but you will find it enjoyable to experiment with them as you learn. Even imperfectly cut sashimi and oddly shaped rolled sushi will taste great, and you will soon find your skills improving.

dashi stock

Dashi stock is the basis of many dishes, so it is often the first item to be prepared in the Japanese kitchen, but, unlike western stocks, it takes only minutes to make. There are several types of dashi to suit different purposes. The three that follow are easy to make and versatile. A subtly aromatic, clear broth, dashi stock enhances and intensifies the flavour of foods it is cooked or blended with. However, it is more than just a stock: it gives a delicate base note to soups, salads, dipping sauces, rice and noodles as well as all kinds of simmered, steamed and stewed foods.

number 1 dashi

This is the most popular variety of dashi, which is made from konbu and bonito fish flakes. A good dashi is delicious enough to eat on its own but requires the best-quality ingredients for a full flavour. This recipe makes 1 litre (1¾ pints).

1 postcard-size piece of konbu
1 litre (1¾ pints) water
20g (¾oz) dried bonito flakes

Wipe off any pieces of dirt from the konbu with damp kitchen paper, then make small tears in it to encourage the maximum release of flavour. Place in a saucepan with the water and bring to the boil over a low heat. Remove the konbu when it begins to float to the surface, just before the water reaches boiling point – do not boil the konbu as it will discolour the dashi and make it taste bitter.

Add the bonito flakes and bring the water back to the boil, then remove from the heat. Allow the flakes to settle to the bottom of the pan, then strain the stock using a fine-meshed sieve lined with kitchen paper or a coffee filter.

The delicate flavour and taste of dashi is lost if it is frozen, so it is best to make the stock fresh each time and use it the same day.

vegetarian dashi

In the traditional Japanese kitchen, vegetarian dashi is made from konbu and dried shiitake mushrooms, which give it a subtle smoky flavour. Makes 1 litre (1¾ pints).

2 postcard-size pieces of konbu
3 dried shiitake mushrooms
1 litre (1¾ pints) water

Wipe the konbu clean with damp kitchen paper and make some tears in it to help it to infuse and for the maximum release of flavour. Place the konbu and the mushrooms in a saucepan with the water and leave to soak for at least 1 hour or overnight. Bring slowly to the boil over a low heat.

Remove the konbu when it begins to float to the surface, just before the water reaches boiling point. Turn up the heat and boil rapidly for 2 minutes, then set aside to cool to room temperature. Remove the mushrooms.

As with the number 1 dashi stock, this vegetarian dashi also loses its delicate flavour and aroma if frozen. It is therefore best to make a fresh batch each time you need it and to use it the same day.

water dashi

This flavoursome dashi is the easiest version to prepare; it is not cooked but left to infuse overnight, ready to use the next day. Makes 1 litre (1¾ pints).

1 postcard-size piece of konbu
3 dried shiitake mushrooms
7g (¼oz) dried bonito flakes
1 litre (1¾ pints) water (boiled tap water or bottled spring water)

Wipe the konbu clean with damp kitchen paper and make some tears in it to help it to infuse and for the maximum release of flavour. Put all the dry ingredients in a glass jug with a lid or sealable plastic container and add the water. Chill in the refrigerator overnight and strain before use. The dashi will keep up for up to three days in the refrigerator.

how to cook rice

Rice is the staple of the Japanese diet, and no matter how elaborate a meal may be, the main course always includes a bowl of rice. Although domestic production and consumption have been on the decline for some decades due to the ever-increasing westernisation of Japanese life, this humble grain still holds centre stage in the Japanese kitchen. American-grown, Japanese-style, short-grain rice is widely available outside Japan and is the closest substitute for home-grown rice. Typically sold in 1kg (2¼lb) or 2.5kg (5½lb) packages, it is usually labelled 'Japanese-style' or 'sushi' rice.

Today, nearly all Japanese households have automatic electric or gas rice cookers complete with electric timers, a choice of programmes, thermal control and options such as delayed start, and they are used at least once a day for preparing family meals. An electric rice cooker is a labour-saving, fail-safe piece of kitchen equipment, and will deliver consistently good results – if you often eat rice it is well worth buying one. But you can also cook perfect Japanese rice without an automatic rice cooker.

For rice with a subtly sweet taste, which is plump, glossy and slightly sticky (so that it is easy to eat with chopsticks), you need to wash off the starch that coats the surface of the raw grain before you begin cooking.

Below you will find two methods for cooking and preparing 'Japanese-style' rice: the first method is for making rice that is to be eaten on its own, to be fried or to accompany other dishes (such as donburi or curry); the second method is for making rice for sushi (such as maki, nigiri, hand rolls, and inside-out rolls).

cooking rice for non-sushi dishes

Measure the rice into a large bowl and add plenty of cold water. Stir vigorously, then drain the milky water through a fine-meshed sieve. Return the rinsed rice to the bowl and repeat until the water runs clear. The rice will need between 3 and 5 washes before the rinsing water runs clear and will become slightly opaque as it begins to absorb moisture. Leave the rice in the sieve to continue draining for at least 1 hour before cooking. If you are short of time you can leave the rice to soak in the saucepan with the water for cooking (see below) for 10–15 minutes before you turn on the heat. A saucepan with a thick base (preferably curved rather than flat) and a tight-fitting, solid lid is ideal.

To cook rice, you will need about 20 per cent more water by volume than dry rice. To serve four people use 300–400g (10–14oz) dry rice and 360–480ml (13–17fl oz) water. Put the washed and drained rice with the measured water into a saucepan over a medium to high heat and bring to the boil. Try to resist the temptation to lift the lid to see how it is cooking, as you want to keep all the steam inside – listen for boiling sounds instead. Depending on the amount of rice you are cooking, it should take between 5 and 7 minutes to reach a rolling boil. Reduce the heat to low and continue to cook for a further 5–7 minutes before turning off the heat. Do not lift the lid but let the rice stand for 10 minutes to cook in its own steam.

With a moistened spatula, turn the cooked rice over from the bottom to fluff it up, and place a tea towel under the lid to absorb the steam and prevent it cooking further while you are waiting to serve.

YO! Sushi tips

- A golden-coloured crust sometimes forms on the bottom of cooked rice. This is the equivalent of the crusty heel of a loaf and it can be broken up and distributed through the white rice or set aside to eat later with a sprinkling of salt.
- Rice is an annual plant typically harvested in the autumn in the northern hemisphere. In Japan, newly harvested rice – *shin mai* – comes on to the market from September to November. The American equivalent is often labelled as 'new harvest rice', distinguishing it from previous years' rice crops. Newly harvested rice is sweet and contains more moisture, so it needs less water to cook.

cooking and preparing sushi rice

Good sushi begins with good sushi rice. Of course, the quality and freshness of the fish is paramount, but the importance of the sushi rice is often overlooked. At sushi restaurants, *su-meshi*, (literally, vinegar-flavoured rice) is called *shari* – an esoteric reference to the bones of Buddha, which reflects the importance of sushi rice in Japanese food culture.

To prepare sushi rice, you need less water than when cooking normal, plain-boiled rice because vinegar is added after cooking. The ratio of rice to water is 10 per cent more water than rice. See the chart below for quantities. To help the rice to cook through it must have absorbed moisture before cooking, so it is vital that the rice is washed and set aside for at least 1 hour before cooking. To make perfect sushi rice follow the 3 steps below.

step 1: boiling the rice

Measure the rice and pour into a large bowl. Add plenty of cold water and stir vigorously, then drain the milky water through a fine-meshed sieve. Return the rinsed rice to the bowl and repeat until the water runs clear. The rice will need between 3 and 5 washes before the rinsing water runs clear and will become slightly opaque as it begins to absorb moisture. Set it aside to drain for at least 1 hour.

Put the rice and the measured amount of water (see the first table overleaf) into a heavy-based saucepan with a tight-fitting lid and add a postcard-size piece of konbu into which you have made little tears. (The konbu is optional but it does give extra flavour to the rice.)

sushi rice and water quantities

raw rice	+	water	=	cooked rice
200g (7oz)		220ml (8fl oz)		300g (10oz)
400g (14oz)		440ml (16fl oz)		600g (1¼lb)
500g (1lb 2oz)		550ml (19fl oz)		750g (1½lb)
600g (1¼lb)		660ml (23fl oz)		900g (2lb)
1kg (2¼lb)		1.1 litre (2 pints)		1.5kg (3lb 5oz)

Put the saucepan over a medium to high heat and bring to the boil. Try to resist the temptation to lift the lid to see how it is cooking, as you want to keep all the steam inside – listen for boiling sounds instead. Depending on the amount of rice you are cooking, it should take between 5 and 7 minutes to reach a rolling boil. Reduce the heat to low and continue to cook for a further 5–7 minutes before turning off the heat. Do not lift the lid but let the rice stand for 10 minutes to cook in its own steam. The next step is to make the sushi vinegar.

step 2: making the sushi vinegar

Sushi vinegar is added to cooked rice while it is still hot to create sushi rice. Although it can be bought in Japanese stores it is more economical to make your own and the flavour will be superior. The amount of sugar varies, depending on personal taste and what the vinegar will be used for. Generally speaking, a less-sweet vinegar mixture is suitable for raw fish whereas more strongly flavoured or cooked ingredients such as grilled eel, marinated mackerel, eggs and seasoned vegetables require a sweeter sushi vinegar.

cooked rice, rice vinegar, sugar and salt quantities

cooked rice	rice vinegar	sugar	salt
300g (10oz)	30ml (1fl oz)	15–30g (¾–1½oz)	1½ tsp
600g (1¼lb)	60ml (2fl oz)	30–60g (1½–2¼oz)	12g (½oz)
750g (1½lb)	75ml (3fl oz)	40–75g (1½–3oz)	20g (¾oz)
900g (2lb)	90ml (3½fl oz)	45–90g (2–3½oz)	25g (1oz)
1.5kg (3lb 5oz)	150ml (5fl oz)	75–150g (3–5oz)	40g (1½oz)

To make sushi vinegar, combine the rice vinegar, sugar and salt in a non-metallic bowl and stir well until the sugar and salt have dissolved.

step 3: mixing the rice and sushi vinegar together

In Japan a broad and shallow cedarwood tub called a *hangiri* is used to mix sushi rice. It is hard to find outside Japan, however, and a shallow wooden salad bowl with a flat base makes an excellent substitute. Alternatively use a shallow, flat-based dish. You will also need a spatula (a flat wooden one is ideal) and a hand-held fan, although a piece of cardboard or a magazine will do.

Transfer the hot cooked rice to a moistened bowl or dish and use a moistened spatula to break up the mound of rice and to spread it evenly in the bowl or dish. Using the back of the spatula, sprinkle the sushi vinegar mixture over the rice (see opposite for quantity of vinegar to rice). Use the spatula to cut through the rice and turn it over in sections to distribute the vinegar throughout. Hold the fan in one hand as you turn the rice using the other, fanning it to cool it as quickly as possible. (This is easier if you have someone who can fan the rice for you as you turn it.) The rice will become glossy as it absorbs the vinegar mixture. Do not stir or mix the rice – this will make it mushy.

If you are not making sushi straight away, cover the rice with a dampened tea towel to stop it drying out and stand it in a cool part of the kitchen out of direct sunlight.

Prepared sushi rice will keep at room temperature for up to 4 hours – use the same day and do not refrigerate.

how to cook noodles

Noodles are very popular in Japan. Japanese people regularly eat huge quantities of soba, udon, somen and ramen, both at home and in noodle shops, at any time of the day or year. Whatever the size of the serving, noodles are never considered more than a quick bite or part of a main meal. In fact, noodles make an ideal snack as they are quick and easy to prepare, highly versatile, instantly satisfying and very digestible.

Dried and semi-dried noodles in vacuum packs are now widely available outside Japan, so are good store-cupboard standbys. Dried noodles tend to come in bundles neatly tied with paper ribbons making it easy to estimate serving portions. The Japanese prefer their noodles to have *koshi*, which literally means 'a hip', although in a culinary context it means having a good texture – just as the Italians like their pasta *al dente* (tender with just a little bite). Unlike pasta, however, noodles have to be cooked through to the centre, but the outside must not become sticky and soft. Noodles cannot be cooked in advance – they have to be eaten straight away otherwise they become soggy. Compared to pasta, noodles take almost no time to cook, so you must have everything else ready before you start. The following method will give you successful results every time.

Bring a large saucepan of water to a rolling boil over a medium to high heat. Untie the ribbons, if the noodles are tied, and drop in the noodles, giving them a quick stir with a chopstick to separate them. Stand by with half a glass of cold water and watch the pan. As soon as the cooking water begins to rise and is about to boil over, pour in the cold water. This will reduce the temperature of the cooking water so that the middle of each noodle cooks at the same speed as the outside. Depending on the thickness and dryness of the noodles, you may have to repeat this.

To test if the noodles are done, lift out a strand and take a bite. Ideally the noodle will be tender all the way through, with no hard core, and the outside will be slippery without being too soggy. If you are making a large quantity, cook the noodles in batches and use a sieve or strainer to scoop out cooked noodles so you don't have to pour away the cooking water. Whether serving noodles hot or cold, the Japanese rinse their noodles under cold running water to wash off the surface starch and then drain them well.

choosing fish

Many of the most popular dishes at YO! Sushi include raw fish. This must
be perfectly fresh and of the highest quality. Buying good-quality, 'sushi-
grade' fish is the first step in making delicious sushi, so it is always a good
idea to get to know your local fishmonger. Good fishmongers are generally
more than happy to talk about their fish and are pleased to give you advice.
Instead of asking if the fish is fresh, ask how fresh it is or when it was caught,
and also ask what they recommend. Tell your fishmonger that you are making
sushi or sashimi. They will advise you on their fish and tell you if it is suitable
to be eaten raw.

   When it comes to choosing a fish, a whole fish gives more clues about
its freshness than a cut: the eyes should be clear, not cloudy, and they should
be plump, not sunken. Look behind the gills – they should be bright red, not
dark blood-red. The skin should be glossy and the flesh should feel firm and
springy to the touch, free of any cuts or bruises. Fresh fish smells pleasantly
of the sea.

   Although judging the freshness of cut pieces is more difficult, the same
principles apply – look, touch and smell. Generally, avoid buying pre-packed
cuts in supermarkets, as it is very difficult to tell how fresh the fish is and
how it has been handled. Finally, remember to tell your fishmonger if you are
making sushi or sashimi and ask them to prepare the fish for you. All good
suppliers will fillet the fish for you, and may even cut it into pieces if you ask.

how to slice fish for sashimi and sushi

slicing fillets for sashimi

1

Hold a sharp knife with your index finger placed on the back of the blade. Cut along the line of the spine and cut off the narrow tail end.

2

Trim off any darker meat or skin that is left. Take one fillet and turn it horizontally on the chopping board. Hold it in place with one hand.

3

Tilt the blade at a 60 degree angle to the fish. Gently cut down to a thickness of just under 1cm (½in).

slicing steaks for sashimi

1

Place the skinless steak on a chopping board. Holding it securely in position, cut the steak in half.

2

Take one half of the steak and turn it 90 degree so that it is horizontal on the board. Tilt the blade at a 60 degree angle to the fish and cut down to a thickness of just under 1cm (1/2in).

slicing strips for rolled sushi

Place the fillet lengthways on the chopping board and, with the blade at a 90 degree angle, cut into 1cm (1/2in)-wide sticks.

how to make hand rolls

1

Fold and tear a nori sheet into two rectangles of equal size.

Hold a piece of nori in one hand with the smooth-side down.

2

Take a generous tablespoon of prepared sushi rice and put it on the left side of the nori.

With the back of the spoon, spread the rice roughly into a downward-pointing triangle. Now stick 2–3 grains of rice on the bottom right-hand corner of the nori – this is to help seal the handroll later.

3

Smear a dab of wasabi paste in the middle of the triangle.

Place your chosen fillings diagonally across the centre of the triangle allowing the fillings to stick out at the top left-hand corner.

4

Lift the bottom left-hand corner of the nori with your right hand and fold it over the fillings to meet the middle of the top edge.

5

Continue rolling until the nori forms a cornet shape.

6

Use the grains of rice that you stuck on earlier to seal the nori.

how to make maki

1

Put a rolling mat on top of a chopping board in front of you. Fold and tear a nori sheet in half and place one half on the mat shiny-side down. Leave a 1cm (½in) gap at the bottom edge of the rolling mat. Wet your hands in a bowl of lightly vinegared water.

2

Take a handful of prepared sushi rice – about 65g (2¼oz) – and mould the rice into a sausage shape .

Place the rice on the nori and, using both hands, spread the rice evenly, leaving a 1cm (½in) margin at the top end of the nori uncovered. Tidy up both the left and right edges of the rice.

3

Press down across the centre of the rice to make a trench for the filling.

Smear a dab of wasabi paste along the trench and place a pencil-shaped filling of your choice on top.

Lift the near edge of the rolling mat and fold it over the filling (holding the filling in place with your middle and ring fingers), aiming to meet the top edge of the rice.

4 Lift the mat slightly to uncover the roll and remove your fingers from inside the roll. Continue to roll until the two edges of the nori meet.

5 Cover the roll with the rolling mat again and gently press to shape it into a neat, square-sided roll.

6 Wet a kitchen knife with water to stop the rice from sticking to it.

Place the roll on a chopping board and cut it in the middle. Lay the two halves parallel to each other and cut both of them into three pieces of equal length so that you have six pieces.

how to make
inside-out rolls (ISO)

1 Wrap a sushi rolling mat in a large piece of cling film to cover both sides. Place half a sheet of nori on the mat, 1cm (½in) from the bottom edge.

Wet your hands in a bowl of lightly vinegared water. Take a large handful of prepared sushi rice, about 175g (6oz), and shape it into a sausage.

2 Put the rice on the centre of the nori and spread it so that it covers the whole of the nori evenly. Try not to press down too hard, as this will make the finished ISO dense and heavy.

3 Flip the rice-covered nori over so that the nori is on top. Then place your chosen fillings across the centre of the nori.

4

Lift up the edge of the rolling mat with your thumbs and index fingers while holding the fillings in position with your middle and ring fingers.

5

Roll it away from you to form a cylinder of uniform thickness.

Cover the ISO with the rolling mat and gently squeeze along the length of the roll.

6

Uncover the ISO. If you wish to coat it with sesame seeds or roe, spread the seeds or roe on a plate and roll the ISO in them.

To cut the roll, moisten a sharp knife and cut in half. Place the two halves together, moisten the knife again and cut three times to give eight equally sized pieces.

how to make nigiri

1

Have the prepared sushi rice, wasabi paste and a bowl of cold lightly vinegared water ready.

Pre-cut the sushi toppings of your choice and lay them ready on the chopping board.

Wet your hands with the water to stop the rice sticking. With one hand take a dessertspoon – about 20g (¾oz) – of the prepared rice.

2

Transfer the rice into the other hand and gently roll it in your palm to shape it into an oblong ball.

Place the rice ball on the chopping board and tidy up the shape, taking care not to over-handle it or press it too hard.

3

Smear a dab of wasabi paste on top of the rice ball.

4

Lay the sushi topping on the rice ball.

Gently mould the topping to the rice and check the shape before serving.

preparing cooked prawns for nigiri

1

Take a cooked prawn (see page 184) and peel away the outer shell. Leave the tail intact.

Take a small sharp knife and cut along the underside of the prawn. Don't cut all the way through, but stop when you reach the dark vein. Gently remove the vein.

2

Open up the prawn and, with your index and middle fingers, press down to flatten it. Place the prawn on a rice ball.

how to make gunkan

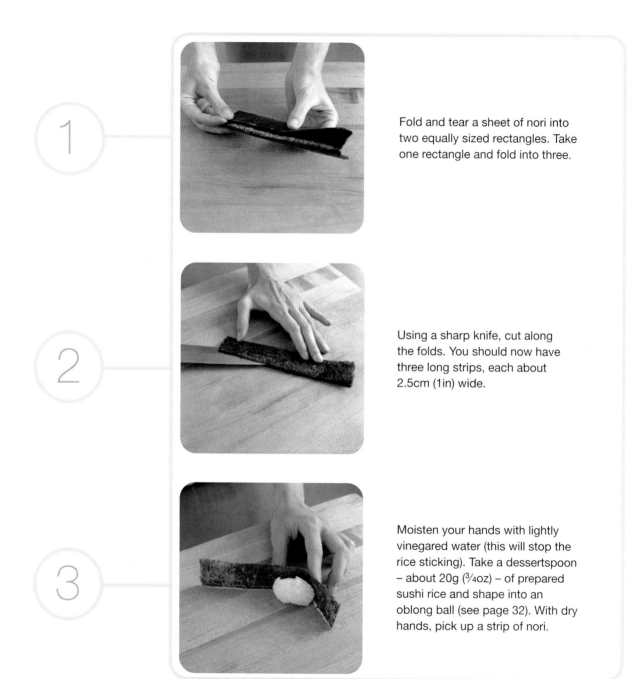

1 Fold and tear a sheet of nori into two equally sized rectangles. Take one rectangle and fold into three.

2 Using a sharp knife, cut along the folds. You should now have three long strips, each about 2.5cm (1in) wide.

3 Moisten your hands with lightly vinegared water (this will stop the rice sticking). Take a dessertspoon – about 20g (¾oz) – of prepared sushi rice and shape into an oblong ball (see page 32). With dry hands, pick up a strip of nori.

4

Wrap the nori around the rice ball with the smooth side of the nori facing outwards.

5

Press a grain of rice on to the end of the nori strip. This will prevent the nori from unravelling.

With your index finger make a slight depression in the top of the rice. Smear a dab of wasabi into the depression.

6

Use a teaspoon to place the filling on top of the rice, keeping it inside the nori ring.

how to make tempura

Tempura batter gives vegetables and fish a light, crispy coating for frying. The batter is best made using special tempura flour, which is available from Japanese grocery stores and large supermarkets. However, if you can't get hold of it, use fine plain flour – do not use strong bread flour, which is too sticky.

   The batter needs to remain as cold as possible, so use ice-cold water to mix it and do not stand the bowl near the hob or any other source of heat. Tempura batter must be freshly made and used immediately. If you make the batter too far in advance or prepare a large quantity the batter will become heavy and sticky while you coat and cook all the portions. Have all the ingredients ready prepared and the oil heated before mixing the batter.

1

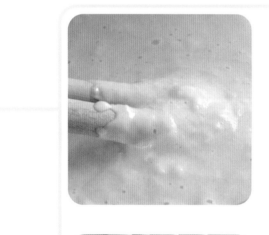

Have your ingredients ready before making up the batter.

Lightly mix the egg with cold water, but do not whisk the mixture. Add the sifted tempura flour to the egg mixture. Using the handles of two wooden spoons or cooking chopsticks (not a whisk or a fork), mix the batter briefly and lightly.

2

It does not matter if there are a few lumps in it. Over-mixing will result in a heavy, sticky batter.

Dip your ingredients into the batter just before frying.

3

Use a heavy-based saucepan (cast-iron or copper is ideal) that will keep the oil at a constant temperature. Fill it three-quarters full with oil.

Test the temperature of the oil by dripping a little batter into it. The batter should sink halfway down before floating back to the surface.

4

If the batter sinks to the bottom and takes a while to float back up, the oil temperature is too low and the batter will not cook to a light crisp; if the batter stays on the surface, the oil is too hot. The oil temperature should be about 170–180°C (325–350°F).

5

Fry the ingredients in small batches. Adding too many will lower the temperature and result in heavy batter.

Drop the ingredients into the oil. Turn over two or three times using cooking chopsticks or tongs. Remove from the oil when crisp and slightly golden.

sauces, dressings and marinades

teriyaki sauce

This is one of the most commonly used sauces in the YO! Sushi kitchen. *Teriyaki* literally means 'to glaze'. The sauce is brushed over a piece of meat or fish while it is grilling. It is particularly suitable for oily fish such as tuna, mackerel or yellowtail and for chicken. You can vary the proportions to suit your taste but the general ratio is 3 portions of soy sauce, 3 portions of mirin, 1 portion each of sake and sugar.

makes about 300ml (10fl oz)

150ml (5fl oz) soy sauce
150ml (5fl oz) mirin
50ml (2fl oz) sake
50ml (2fl oz) sugar

Mix all the ingredients together in a shallow saucepan and bring to the boil over a medium heat, stirring to ensure that all the sugar is dissolved. Reduce the heat to low and let the mixture simmer for a further 15–20 minutes or until the liquid has been reduced by a third and is syrupy and glossy. Let the sauce cool down completely before transferring it to a glass jar. Seal and store for up to 4 weeks in the refrigerator.

yakitori sauce

This is another versatile sauce that can be used not only to make delicious, succulent yakitori but also as a noodle sauce or marinade. You can make the sauce even more versatile by mixing it with curry powder or a bit of tomato ketchup.

makes about 540ml (18½fl oz)

2 pieces of konbu, 5cm x 5cm (2in x 2in)
240ml (8fl oz) mirin
100ml (3½fl oz) sake
200ml (7fl oz) soy sauce
5g (¼oz) bonito flakes

Place the konbu in a non-stick frying pan and warm over a low heat for 1 minute. This freshens up the konbu and restores its aroma.

Put the mirin and sake in a saucepan and bring to the boil to burn off the alcohol. Add the soy sauce and return to the boil. Remove from the heat, add the bonito flakes and leave to cool to room temperature.

Put the konbu in a glass jar. Line a sieve with kitchen paper or a coffee filter and strain the liquid through into the glass jar. Seal and store in the refrigerator, and use within 2 weeks.

yakisoba sauce

Although *yakisoba* may translate to 'seared soba noodles' it has nothing to do with actual soba noodles: it uses soft, Chinese-style egg noodles that are sold vacuum-packed in supermarkets. Ready-mixed yakisoba sauces are available from Japanese stores but it is far better to mix your own.

makes about 600ml (1 pint)

120ml (4fl oz) soy sauce
240ml (8½fl oz) HP sauce or brown sauce
120ml (4¼fl oz) oyster sauce
60ml (2¼fl oz) rice vinegar
60ml (2¼fl oz) tomato ketchup
60g (2¼oz) soft brown sugar

Combine all the ingredients in a bowl and stir until the sugar has dissolved. Transfer to a bottle and store in a cool, dark kitchen cupboard. Use within a week.

YO! Sushi tip

This recipe uses HP sauce or brown sauce instead of traditional Bulldog sauce, which can be hard to find. If you do have Bulldog sauce, use 240ml (8½fl oz) and omit the HP or brown sauce.

You can use honey instead of soft brown sugar and a dash or two of Tabasco sauce if you prefer your sauces spicy.

gyoza dipping sauce

Gyoza are delectable little dumplings filled with minced vegetable, chicken or prawn (see recipe page 102). They are served with this vinegar soy dipping sauce.

serves 4

2 tbsp rice vinegar
3 tbsp soy sauce
2–3 drops sesame oil

Combine all the ingredients in a mixing bowl, stir, and serve with gyoza dumplings for dipping.

sweet chilli mayonnaise

This delicious sauce is especially good in handrolls and california rolls (see pages 144–146 and 150).

makes 250ml (9fl oz)

200ml (7fl oz) good-quality mayonnaise
50ml (2fl oz) smooth, sweet chilli sauce, widely available from supermarkets

Combine the ingredients thoroughly in a mixing bowl. It is best kept refrigerated in a squeezable plastic bottle. Use within a week.

ginger wasabi mayonnaise

This is an easy mayonnaise-based sauce with a difference. The kick of the wasabi and ginger works well with the creamy richness of the mayonnaise. You can use this in any recipe that calls for wasabi paste, but it is particularly suited to oily fish or meat dishes.

makes about 220g (8oz)

4 tsp wasabi powder
20g (¾oz) fresh root ginger, peeled
200g (7oz) good-quality mayonnaise

Mix the wasabi powder with an equal amount of water to make a runny paste – add a little more water if necessary.

Grate the ginger, then squeeze it between your fingers to extract about 2 teaspoons of juice. Discard the pulp.

Combine the wasabi, ginger juice and mayonnaise to make a pale green mixture. Transfer to a squeezable plastic bottle and keep refrigerated. Use within a week.

tempura dipping sauce

Tempura is a delicious and speedy way to cook fresh vegetables, fish and seafood. Ideally it should be eaten straight away dipped in this subtle sauce.

makes about 450ml (15fl oz)

100ml (3½fl oz) mirin
300ml (10fl oz) dashi stock (see pages 16–17)
100ml (3½fl oz) light soy sauce

Put the mirin in a saucepan and bring to the boil over a medium heat. Add the dashi and the soy sauce and return to the boil. Reduce the heat to low and let it simmer gently for 10 minutes to reduce the sauce slightly. Remove from the heat and serve at room temperature.

harusame sauce

This sauce goes well with any noodles, especially Japanese harusame noodles, fine vermicelli noodles or rice sticks.

makes about 400ml (14fl oz)

20g (¾oz) fresh root ginger, peeled
20g (¾oz) garlic cloves
200ml (7fl oz) rice vinegar
200ml (7fl oz) soy sauce
2 heaped tbsp granulated sugar
2 tsp sesame oil

Grate the ginger, then squeeze it between your fingers to extract the juice. Discard the pulp. Grate the garlic cloves and combine with the ginger juice in a small mixing bowl. Add the remaining ingredients and mix well to ensure the sugar is completely dissolved. Store in a sealed jar in the refrigerator. Use within a week.

yuzu marinade

Yuzu is a Japanese citrus fruit which looks like a yellow tangerine. It has a uniquely refreshing taste and aroma. This wonderful marinade works well with any fish, especially salmon or firm, white fish such as bream or sea bass.

makes 300ml (10fl oz)

100ml (3½fl oz) yuzu juice
200ml (7fl oz) rice vinegar
50g (2oz) sugar
1 tbsp salt

Combine all the ingredients in a mixing bowl and stir well to dissolve all the sugar and salt. Boil the marinade for 1 minute before using it for basting. Cook the food well after basting – at least 1 minute.

katsu sauce

serves 4

125ml (4½fl oz) brown or HP sauce
50ml (2fl oz) tomato ketchup
1 tbsp runny honey

Put the brown sauce, tomato ketchup and honey into a small bowl and mix well.

Keep refrigerated and use within 2 weeks.

soy dashi

Soy dashi is brilliantly versatile and packed with flavour. Use it as a marinade, a sauce for noodles or a seasoning for hot dishes.

makes about 520ml (18½fl oz)

2 postcard-size pieces konbu
240ml (8½fl oz) mirin
100ml (3½fl oz) sake
200ml (7fl oz) soy sauce
5g (⅛oz) bonito flakes

Place the konbu in a non-stick frying pan and warm over a low heat for 1 minute – this is to restore the flavour of the konbu.

Put the mirin and sake in a saucepan and bring to the boil over a medium heat to burn off the alcohol. Add the soy sauce and bring back to the boil. Remove from the heat, add the bonito flakes and leave to cool to room temperature. Line a sieve with kitchen paper or a coffee filter and strain the sauce straight into a glass storage jar. Discard the bonito. Add the pieces of konbu to the jar and put on the lid. Leave the sauce to infuse overnight before using.

Keep refrigerated and use within 10 days.

garlic soy sauce

This is a marvellously strong sauce and is especially good in quick stir-fries. The added bonus is that once you've used the sauce, you're left with delicious soy-pickled garlic that can be sliced and cooked with other vegetables.

makes about 250ml (9fl oz)

1 whole head of garlic
100ml ($3^1/_2$fl oz) sake
200ml (7fl oz) soy sauce

Peel and halve each garlic clove.

Put the sake in a small saucepan and bring to the boil over a medium heat. Add the soy sauce and return to the boil. Remove from the heat and leave to cool to room temperature. Put the garlic in a glass storage jar and pour in the sauce. Leave for 24–48 hours to infuse before using.

Store in a cool, dark kitchen cupboard and use within 2 weeks.

spicy soy sauce

This is an ideal sauce for those who like their food spicy and is particularly good with meat dishes. You can use it as a dipping sauce or for basting or seasoning. It is quite hot when it is first made but becomes milder after about two weeks. Use larger chillies rather than the small bird's eye variety, which are very fiery.

makes about 300ml (10fl oz)

100ml ($3^1/_2$fl oz) sake
200ml (7fl oz) light soy sauce
5 large red and 5 large green chillies,
    cut lengthways and deseeded
$^1/_2$ lemon, sliced

Put the sake in a small saucepan over a medium heat and bring to the boil. Add the light soy sauce, bring back to the boil, then remove from the heat. Leave the sake and soy sauce mixture to cool down to room temperature. Put the chillies and slices of lemon in a glass jar and pour in the sauce. Seal and store in the refrigerator for up to 2 weeks.

sweet red miso marinade

Miso is made of fermented soybeans mixed with other grains such as rice, wheat or barley. Miso comes in varying shades of brown, ranging from pale cream to almost steely dark brown. This recipe calls for the robust-flavoured red miso, which works particularly well with strongly flavoured ingredients such as mackerel, pork and lamb.

makes about 300ml (10fl oz)

200g (7oz) red miso paste
100ml (3½fl oz) mirin
100g (3½oz) sugar
30ml (1fl oz) sake

Put all the ingredients in a saucepan and bring to the boil over a medium heat, stirring all the time with a wooden spoon. Reduce the heat to low once the mixture begins to boil. Continue to stir and let the mixture reduce to the consistency of thick yogurt, but be careful not to reduce it too much as it will become harder when cold.

Leave to cool to room temperature before transferring to a jar or plastic food container. Seal and store in the refrigerator and use within 8 weeks.

miso and sweet vinegar dressing

Unlike the previous recipe which calls for red miso, this recipe calls for white miso, which is pale cream in colour and has a mild taste. The result is a refreshing yet full-flavoured miso mixture that can be used as a salad dressing. If you find it difficult to get white miso, use any light-coloured miso of your choice.

makes about 220ml (8fl oz)

30ml (1fl oz) sake
200g (7oz) white miso paste
100ml (3½fl oz) rice vinegar
30g (1oz) sugar

Put the sake in a small saucepan and bring to the boil over a medium heat to burn off the alcohol. Boil the sake rapidly for 1–2 minutes then reduce the heat to low. Add the other ingredients and stir well with a wooden spoon until the sugar has dissolved and the mixture has the consistency of thick cream. Remove from the heat and leave to cool to room temperature before transferring to a jar or plastic food container. Store in the refrigerator and use within 1 month.

sanbaizu

Sanbai means 'three times'. Equal amounts of sugar and soy sauce are combined with three times as much rice vinegar. It is delicious on seafood salads.

makes about 220ml (8fl oz)

50g (2oz) sugar
50ml (2fl oz) soy sauce
150ml (5fl oz) rice vinegar
½ tsp salt

Combine all the ingredients and stir well to ensure that all the sugar and salt is dissolved. Transfer to a glass bottle, keep refrigerated and use within 4 weeks.

konbu sushi vinegar

Prepared bottles of sushi vinegar are available in Japanese stores and some supermarkets but this homemade version is tastier and more economical.

makes about 300ml (10fl oz)

1 postcard-size piece konbu
300ml (10fl oz) rice vinegar
100g (3½oz) sugar
2 tsp salt

Place the konbu in a non-stick frying pan and warm over a low heat for 1 minute. Set the konbu aside. Put the remaining ingredients in a non-aluminium saucepan and bring to the boil over a medium heat. Allow to boil rapidly for 1–2 minutes then turn off the heat and leave to cool to room temperature. Put the konbu in a glass jar with a lid and pour in the vinegar mixture. Leave overnight before using.

ponzu dressing

This is a light and tasty salad dressing.

makes about 300ml (10fl oz)

50ml (2fl oz) cider vinegar
50ml (2fl oz) rice vinegar
50ml (2fl oz) lemon juice
50ml (2fl oz) yuzu juice or lime juice
100ml (3½fl oz) soy sauce

Put all the ingredients in a glass jar with a tight-fitting lid and shake well to combine. Keep refrigerated and use within 1 week.

savoury sweet vinegar dressing

This dressing goes particularly well with deep-fried dishes and strongly flavoured foods.

makes about 200ml (7fl oz)

150ml (5fl oz) rice vinegar
50ml (2fl oz) soy sauce
50g (2oz) sugar
5g (⅛oz) bonito flakes

Put the vinegar, soy sauce and sugar in a saucepan and bring to the boil to dissolve the sugar. Remove from the heat, add the bonito flakes and leave to cool to room temperature. Strain the mixture through a sieve lined with kitchen paper or a coffee filter into a glass jar. Discard the fish flakes. Seal and store in the refrigerator and use within 1 week.

wasabi and watercress salad dressing

This is a stunning-looking and refreshing salad dressing that is guaranteed to delight. It uses stalks that would otherwise be discarded so it is also wonderfully frugal.

makes about 300ml (10fl oz)

100g (3$\frac{1}{2}$oz) fresh watercress stalks, roughly chopped
100ml (3$\frac{1}{2}$fl oz) rice vinegar
4 tbsp soy sauce
$\frac{1}{2}$ tbsp sugar
$\frac{1}{2}$ tsp sea salt
1 tbsp wasabi powder
1 tsp ground black pepper
4 tbsp extra virgin olive oil

Put all the ingredients except the olive oil in a blender and process until the mixture is smooth. Don't worry if tiny bits of watercress are still visible. Transfer the mixture to a glass jar with a tight-fitting lid and add the olive oil. Shake vigorously before use. Seal and store in the refrigerator and use within 3 days.

gomadare (sesame dressing)

Sesame seeds have much more flavour when they are heated or crushed. This sauce is packed with flavour and is a favourite on steamed vegetables or drizzled over salads.

makes about 120ml (4$\frac{1}{4}$fl oz)

4 tbsp toasted sesame seeds
1 tsp sugar
a pinch of sea salt
1 tbsp milk chocolate-coloured miso paste
1 tbsp soy sauce
1 tsp rice vinegar
1 tbsp grapeseed oil
1 tsp sesame seed oil

Put the sesame seeds, sugar, salt and miso into a mortar and grind with a pestle until you have a smooth paste. Add the soy sauce and rice vinegar, and continue to grind until the mixture has the consistency of thick double cream. Transfer to a glass jar, add the oils and shake vigorously to mix. Store in the refrigerator and use within 1 week.

novice

easy recipes
to get you started

wakame and cucumber salad

This is a classic dish, known in Japanese as *sunomono*, which literally means 'vinegar-flavoured food'. It is ideal as a healthy starter or side dish.

serves 4

4 heaped tbsp wakame
2 baby cucumbers or 1 regular cucumber
½ tsp salt
10g (a thumb-length piece) fresh ginger, peeled
4–6 tbsp sanbaizu (see page 47)

Start by hydrating the wakame by soaking it in a bowl of cold water for 10 minutes or until it is soft but not soggy – it should be al dente. While the wakame is soaking, slice the baby cucumbers as thinly as possible. If you are using a regular cucumber, peel it and cut it in half lengthways, then scoop or cut out the seedy centre and slice the cucumber as thinly as possible. Whichever size cucumber you are using, soak the slices in a bowl of cold, salted water for 5–8 minutes, then drain them well, using your hands to gently squeeze out any remaining moisture. Drain the softened wakame in the same way.

Cut the peeled ginger into thin shreds. Put the wakame, cucumber and ginger in a bowl and pour the sanbaizu over. Toss well, then divide among 4 dishes and serve.

edamame

Edamame are young green soybeans that are harvested before they are mature and sold frozen still in their hairy pod. They're fun to pull apart to get to the beans inside.

serves 4

200g (7oz) frozen edamame in their pods
¼ tsp sea salt

Bring a large saucepan of water to the boil over a medium heat. Add the edamame, bring the water back to the boil and cook for 3–5 minutes. Drain and rinse under cold running water so that the edamame stay bright green, then drain again, sprinkle with salt and serve.

YO! Sushi tips
Remember not to eat the pods – they're too fibrous. If you like your food hot, sprinkle over a small amount of shichimi togarashi (Japanese seven-spice chilli powder).

chilled soba noodle salad

Noodles originally came from China and have become the second staple in Japan after rice. Chilled soba noodles are a refreshing summer favourite and are often served in a bamboo basket.

serves 4

400g (14oz) dried soba noodles
2 tsp toasted sesame oil
100g (3½oz) watercress
100g (3½oz) red chard leaves
4 spring onions, finely chopped
1 tbsp toasted sesame seeds
1 sheet nori, finely shredded

for the dressing
200ml (7fl oz) soy dashi (see page 44)
2 tsp wasabi paste

Bring a large saucepan of water to a rapid boil and add the soba noodles. Stir to ensure that all the noodle strands are separated. Stand by with a glass of cold water, and as soon as the cooking water rises to the top of the pan pour in the cold water (see page 22 for advice on cooking noodles). Drain the noodles, rinse under cold running water and sprinkle with sesame oil. Toss well and set aside to drain.

To make the dressing, mix together the soy dashi and the wasabi paste. Put the noodles and the salad leaves in a large mixing bowl and toss to mix. Divide the noodle salad among 4 plates. Drizzle the dressing over the salad, garnish with the chopped spring onions, sesame seeds and shredded nori. Serve immediately.

YO! Sushi tip

You can vary the amount of soba noodles to suit your appetite and needs – the quantity given here is intended for lunch or a light supper. Also vary the amount of wasabi paste according to taste – remembering that you can always increase the heat, so start with less and add more.

aubergine with ginger ponzu

Known in Japan as *yakinasu,* this classic dish is particularly popular during the hot summer. Aubergines are known to be a cooling vegetable, helping to bring down fevers and promote healthy circulation. A combination of oily aubergines with refreshing ginger and ponzu makes this a perfect starter or side salad – serve it chilled in wine glasses in the summer. Allow half an aubergine per person. If you don't have ponzu handy, use either rice vinegar or lemon juice and soy sauce.

serves 4

2 aubergines
4 tbsp fresh root ginger, peeled and grated
8 tbsp ponzu dressing (see page 47)

Preheat the oven to 220°C/425°F/gas mark 7 and prick the aubergines with a fork or a bamboo skewer – this stops them from exploding in the oven. Line a baking tray with a sheet of foil, lay the aubergines on the foil and bake for 20 minutes or until they feel soft, turning them two or three times. Meanwhile, chill 4 wine glasses or small plates.

Remove the aubergines from the oven and let them cool down enough to handle. Holding the top of the aubergine, insert a bamboo skewer just under the skin and slide it along the length of the aubergine – the skin and the flesh should separate easily. Roughly chop the aubergines and divide among the chilled wine glasses or plates. Chill for 30 minutes or until needed. Put a tablespoon of the grated ginger in the centre of the aubergines, drizzle over the ponzu dressing and serve.

green beans in nutty sesame sauce

Sesame seeds burst with flavour when they are heated or crushed. If you can't get ready-toasted sesame seeds, use raw sesame seeds, which are flatter in shape and lighter in colour. Simply dry-roast the raw seeds in a non-stick frying pan over a medium heat, shaking the pan regularly, for 5–7 minutes or until they are golden and aromatic.

serves 4

200g (7oz) fine green beans, trimmed
½ tsp salt
1 tsp toasted sesame seeds, to garnish

for the sesame sauce
4 tbsp toasted sesame seeds
1–2 tsp sugar
1 tsp light-coloured miso paste
1 tbsp soy sauce

Put the beans on a chopping board and sprinkle them with salt. Gently roll them with your hands – this will ensure they keep their bright green colour when cooked – then place them in a steamer and steam for 2–3 minutes.

To make the sesame sauce, put the sesame seeds in a mortar and grind coarsely with a pestle. Add the sugar and miso paste and grind a little more before pouring in the soy sauce. Continue grinding until the sauce has the consistency of thick yogurt.

Place the beans in a bowl, add the dressing and toss to coat. Serve in a shallow dish, sprinkled with more sesame seeds.

YO! Sushi tip
This sesame seed dressing works well with other cooked vegetables such as broccoli, cauliflower and Brussels sprouts.

tofu and rocket salad with spicy sesame dressing

Tofu is a highly versatile, healthy food that can be combined with practically anything. This is a quick and easy salad that is rich in flavour and texture.

serves 4

200g (7oz) soft silken tofu
1 white or red onion, peeled and thinly sliced
240g (8½oz) rocket leaves
2 tbsp toasted black sesame seeds, to garnish

for the dressing
2 tbsp soy sauce
2 tbsp rice vinegar
2 tsp sesame oil
4 tbsp olive oil
1 tsp ground black pepper
2 tsp chilli sauce
½ tsp crushed garlic

Drain the tofu by wrapping it in kitchen paper and leaving it to stand for 15–20 minutes. Meanwhile, soak the onion in a bowl of cold water to remove the strong smell, then drain well. Cut the tofu into 3cm (1¼in) cubes.

Mix all the dressing ingredients together in a lidded jar and shake well. Arrange the tofu cubes, rocket leaves and onion slices in a large salad bowl. Dress just before serving and sprinkle with the toasted sesame seeds.

YO! Sushi tips
Use a white-skinned onion, if possible, not a cooking onion. Although the tofu needs to be drained, do not over-drain as this will spoil the taste and texture.

Try this recipe with mizuna or watercress, both of which have a crunchy texture and peppery taste.

To make a warm salad for colder months, heat the two oils separately before mixing the dressing.

farmers' miso

This hearty recipe makes a one-bowl meal for two – a perfect choice for a nourishing lunch or a simple supper with salad.

serves 2 as main dish or 4 as starter

½ tbsp vegetable oil
½ onion, finely chopped
2 tbsp pancetta or 4 rashers streaky bacon, finely chopped
4 leaves Savoy cabbage, hard stem removed and roughly chopped
4 tbsp canned chopped tomato
100g (3½oz) can cannellini beans, rinsed and drained
600ml (1 pint) water
2 tbsp tomato purée
4 tbsp milk chocolate-coloured miso paste
salt and ground black pepper
2 tbsp finely chopped parsley, to garnish

Heat the oil in a large saucepan over a medium heat, reduce the heat to low and add the chopped onion. Cover the pan and let the onion sweat for 2–3 minutes until it is soft and golden. Remove the lid and turn up the heat a little. Add the pancetta or bacon and fry until crisp. Add the cabbage, tomato and beans, and cook for 2–3 minutes or until the cabbage is soft, stirring occasionally, then add the water.

Bring to the boil while scooping out any scum that floats to the surface. Once the soup starts to boil, reduce the heat and replace the lid, then simmer for 10 minutes. Put the tomato purée and miso into a small bowl, add a ladleful of liquid from the soup and stir with a fork until all the miso paste is dissolved and you have a yogurt-like mixture. Pour the mixture into the soup and bring slowly back to just below boiling point. Remove from the heat.

Adjust the seasoning with salt and pepper, divide between 2 large soup bowls, garnish with parsley and serve.

YO! Sushi tip
If you're not keen on cabbage, you can use broccoli instead.

miso soup with seaweed, tofu and spring onion

Tasty and comforting, miso soup is packed with easily digestible vegetable protein, vitamin E and various minerals. It is hard to overstate the health benefits of miso (see pages 12–13). Millions of Japanese people start their working day with a bowl of miso soup – it is a healthy breakfast that is quick and easy to make.

serves 4

50g (2oz) tofu of your choice (see right)
4 tbsp wakame
1 litre (1¾ pints) dashi stock (see page 16)
6 heaped tbsp milk chocolate-coloured miso paste
4 spring onions, finely chopped diagonally

Tofu comes in two varieties: the soft silken or firm 'cotton' type. Nutritionally they are the same. While the firm cotton variety is good for stir-frying, the soft silken type is typically eaten on its own or added to soups. Whichever variety you choose for this recipe, you need to drain it by wrapping it in kitchen paper and allowing it to stand for 15–20 minutes. While the tofu is draining, soak the wakame in a bowl of tepid water until it becomes soft but not overly soggy, about 10 minutes.

Heat the dashi stock in a large saucepan over a medium heat but do not let it come to the boil. Dice the drained tofu into 1cm (½in) pieces and drain the softened wakame. Add both to the simmering dashi stock. You cannot add the miso paste directly to the saucepan, as it will not dissolve. Instead, put the miso in a small bowl, add a ladleful of the hot stock and stir with a fork until you have a runny yogurt-like mixture. Stir the miso mixture into the soup. Turn up the heat slightly to return the soup to just below boiling point, then remove from the heat, add the chopped spring onions and serve hot.

YO! Sushi tips
Try using other vegetables such as asparagus or shiitake mushrooms but allow them to cook in the soup for 3 minutes. If you are a vegetarian, use vegetarian dashi stock (see page 17).

miso soup with clams

This easy variation on miso soup has the fresh taste of the sea. The clams make their own flavoursome stock, so there is no need to make dashi stock.

serves 4

350g (12oz) fresh clams or mussels, cleaned (see tip)
600ml (1 pint) water
4–6 tbsp milk chocolate-coloured miso paste
2 spring onions, finely chopped diagonally
sprinkling of shichimi togarashi (Japanese seven-spice chilli powder), to garnish

Put the clams in a saucepan with the water and bring to the boil over a high heat. Turn the heat down once the water begins to boil and cook for a further 5–6 minutes, scooping out any bits that float to the surface.

Put the miso in a small bowl, add a ladleful of the hot clam stock and stir with a fork until you have a runny yogurt-like mixture. Meanwhile, warm 4 soup dishes in the oven. Add the miso mixture to the saucepan and bring the soup back to just below boiling point. Drop in the spring onions and turn off the heat. Discard any clams that remain closed. Ladle the soup into the warm soup bowls, arrange the clams in the centre, garnish with the shichimi togarashi and serve.

YO! Sushi tip
To clean clams, first discard any open or broken shells. Lay them overnight in the refrigerator on sheets of kitchen paper that you've dampened with salted water. This will make them spit out any sand. Wash them in slightly salted water before cooking.

chicken noodle soup

This is a tasty combination of tender chicken and soba noodles that is easy to prepare. Ideally the stock should be made the day before or several hours earlier, so that the flavours can develop. It makes an excellent hearty starter or satisfying one-bowl meal.

serves 4

2 chicken legs
800ml (1½ pints) water
1 carrot, peeled and thinly sliced
400g (14oz) daikon (Japanese white radish), thinly sliced
20g (¾oz) fresh root ginger, peeled and thinly sliced into matchsticks
4 tbsp wakame
1 square of konbu, 10cm x 10cm (4in x 4in)
200ml (7fl oz) light soy sauce
4 tbsp mirin
400g (14oz) dried soba noodles
4 spring onions, finely chopped, to garnish

Put the chicken legs into a large saucepan with the water and add the carrot, daikon and ginger. Bring to the boil over a medium heat, then simmer gently for 20–30 minutes, skimming off any scum that floats to the surface. Turn off the heat and let the stock cool to room temperature, leaving the chicken and vegetables in the stock to keep the chicken moist and tender.

Soak the wakame in a bowl of tepid water for 10 minutes.

Take the chicken out of the stock, put the konbu in, and bring the stock slowly to the boil. Meanwhile, separate the skin and bones from the chicken meat. Retain the meat and discard the skin and bones.

Remove the konbu when the stock begins to boil, then add the soy sauce and mirin. Add the drained wakame. Bring the soup back to the boil for 1–2 minutes, then turn off the heat. Keep the soup warm while you cook the noodles in a separate saucepan as described on page 22. Divide the noodles among 4 serving bowls.

Shred the meat with a fork and put a little onto each portion of noodles. Ladle over the soup, garnish with the chopped spring onions and serve immediately.

mushroom miso soup

A bowl of miso soup served with steaming rice is the simplest but most quintessential example of Japanese home cooking. The flavour of the soup varies and is determined by the intensity of the dashi stock, your choice of miso paste and the proportions of the other ingredients. The sweeter light miso paste used here sets off the earthiness of the mushrooms.

serves 4

4 dried shiitake mushrooms
100 ml (3½fl oz) hot water
700ml (1¼ pint) dashi stock (see page 16)
1 cluster fresh shimeji mushrooms, about
   150g (5oz)
1 cluster fresh enoki mushrooms, about 150g (5oz)
1 leek, trimmed and thinly sliced
40g (1½oz) light-coloured miso paste
dark soy sauce, for seasoning (optional)

Start by soaking the shiitake mushrooms in the hot water for 10–15 minutes, then squeeze them out, discarding the stalks and slicing the caps thinly. In a saucepan, combine the shiitake and their soaking liquor with the dashi stock.

Cut off the bases of the shimeji and enoki mushrooms and separate them. Add to the saucepan with the leek and heat gently. Be careful not to let the soup boil – it should do no more than simmer for 5 minutes to cook the mushrooms and leek.

Put the miso in a small mixing bowl and ladle in a small amount of the soup to soften it. Mix with a fork, then tip the miso mixture back into the saucepan. Turn off the heat as soon as the soup has boiled.

Adjust the seasoning with soy sauce if required, then ladle the soup into 4 serving bowls and serve immediately.

zen vegetable chowder

Zen is the austere Buddhist sect that arrived in Japan from China in the late twelfth century, bringing with it a strict vegan cuisine called *shojin ryori*. Zen monks and nuns observe *shojin ryori* as part of their training. It not only limits cooking and eating to vegetables and seaweed but also dictates one's style of cooking and attitude towards food. Cleanliness and appreciation of food are vital, as is a minimum of wastage. You don't have to become a Zen monk to appreciate these teachings – for the modern cook, this recipe is a perfect way to use up whatever vegetables are languishing in the fridge.

serves 4

1 carrot, scrubbed
1 potato, scrubbed
100g (3½oz) cauliflower
100g (3½oz) broccoli
100g (3½oz) French beans
1 tbsp vegetable oil
½ tsp sesame oil
600ml (1 pint) vegetarian dashi stock (see page 17)
1 tbsp soy sauce
1 tbsp mirin
2 tbsp cornflour, mixed into a paste with
   1 tbsp cold water

Cut the carrot into small pieces. Dice the unpeeled potato finely. Cut the cauliflower and broccoli into small bite-size chunks and the French beans into 1cm (½in) lengths.

Heat the oils in a large saucepan for 1–2 minutes over a medium heat, then add all the vegetables. Stir them gently for 5–7 minutes.

Add the dashi stock and turn the heat up to high until the stock is almost boiling. Reduce the heat to low and let it simmer for 5 minutes. Add the soy sauce and mirin. Add the cornflour paste, stir and bring the stock back to just below boiling point. Serve immediately.

YO! Sushi tip

Try using seasonal vegetables: asparagus and sugar snaps in the spring, courgettes and runner beans in the summer, sweet potatoes, pumpkins or squash in the autumn, leeks and parsnips in the winter.

potato salad with wasabi mayonnaise

Many dishes that appear regularly on the Japanese table have foreign origins but have been adapted to suit a Japanese palate. The humble potato salad is a very good example of a western recipe that has been given a Japanese twist.

serves 4

450g (1lb) new potatoes or a waxy variety such
    as Charlotte or Maris Bard, peeled
½ carrot, peeled
1 baby cucumber
1 red shallot or ½ red onion, very finely chopped
50g (2oz) sliced ham, cut into small strips 2.5cm
    (1in) long (optional)
1 handful of flat-leaf parsley, finely chopped,
    to garnish

for the wasabi mayonnaise
1 tsp wasabi powder
2 tsp rice vinegar (or cider vinegar)
150g (5oz) good-quality mayonnaise

Cut the potatoes into 2cm (¾in) cubes. Chop the carrot into 1cm (½in) dice. Bring a large saucepan of water to the boil, cook the potato for 5 minutes, then add the carrot, bring back to the boil and cook for a further 3 minutes. Drain, rinse under cold running water and set aside to drain again. Meanwhile, cut the cucumber in half lengthways, scoop out the seedy part in the centre with a teaspoon and thinly slice.

To make the wasabi mayonnaise, mix the wasabi powder with the rice or cider vinegar in a large, non-metallic mixing bowl and stir in the mayonnaise. Add the potato, carrot, shallot or onion, ham (if using) and cucumber to the bowl. Toss to coat well with the wasabi mayonnaise, then let the salad stand for at least 15 minutes to allow the vegetables to absorb the flavour of the mayonnaise. Garnish with the chopped parsley before serving.

okonomiyaki (savoury japanese pancake)

The literal translation of *okonomiyaki* is 'choice toast', an apt name for a popular Japanese street snack. It's the Japanese equivalent of a crêpe or pizza and is eaten on its own as a snack or light meal. Like both of these European dishes, okonomiyaki can be filled with whatever you choose.

serves 4 as a main meal, 6 as a snack

600g (1¼lb) Savoy or pointed cabbage, shredded
1 leek, cut in half lengthways and thinly sliced
1 carrot, peeled and shredded
100g (3½oz) beansprouts, trimmed of their roots
20g (¾oz) fresh root ginger, peeled and grated
4 tbsp plain flour
1 tsp salt
2 tbsp water
4 medium eggs
1 tbsp vegetable oil
200g (7oz) cooked shelled prawns
½ sheet nori, crushed, to garnish

Put all the vegetables and the ginger in a large mixing bowl, add the flour, salt, water and eggs, and mix well. Heat a large non-stick frying pan over a medium heat, add the oil and cook the vegetable mixture for 5–7 minutes or until the underside is cooked and firm.

Lay the prawns over the uncooked top side, then turn the pancake over to cook for a further 4–6 minutes. If you are not confident enough to flip the pancake, put the whole pan under a hot grill for 4–6 minutes or until firm and lightly browned. Transfer the pancake to a chopping board, cut into wedges, garnish with crushed nori and serve.

Chicken yakitori is one of YO! Sushi's most popular dishes. Even Japanese people find it hard to resist the tempting aroma of yakitori wafting down the street. A tasty starter or canapé, it is easy to make and can be prepared in advance.

serves 4

8 bamboo skewers
200g (7oz) chicken thighs, skinned and boned
100ml (3½fl oz) yakitori sauce (see page 40)
4 baby leeks or 8 spring onions (white part only)
sprinkling of shichimi togarashi (Japanese
    seven-spice chilli powder)
1 handful of cos lettuce leaves, to serve (optional)

Before you start, soak the bamboo skewers in water for at least 30 minutes – this is to stop them from burning during cooking. Cut the chicken thighs into small bite-size cubes (allow 4 cubes per skewer) and leave to marinate in the yakitori sauce for 15–20 minutes.

While the chicken is marinating, preheat the oven to 190°C/375°F/gas mark 5 and chop the baby leeks or spring onions into 24 4cm (1½in)-long pieces (3 pieces per skewer).

Remove the chicken pieces from the marinade and pat them dry with kitchen paper, reserving the marinade.

Pour the leftover marinade into a small saucepan. Bring to the boil, reduce the heat and simmer for 3–4 minutes. Turn off the heat.

Dry the bamboo skewers. Divide the chicken and leek into 8, then thread alternate pieces of chicken and leek onto each skewer. Line a baking tray with foil, lay a grill rack on top and cook the skewers for 5 minutes on each side, basting them with the marinade from time to time. Sprinkle over the shichimi togarashi and serve on a bed of lettuce.

YO! Sushi tip
You can also use asparagus spears instead of leeks when they are in season.

green tea prawns with cucumber salsa

The health benefits of green tea are well known: it helps to lower blood pressure and is good for your skin. In addition to drinking it, use it in your cooking to add a delicate flavour to dishes.

serves 4

20 large raw prawns
500ml (18fl oz) water
4 good-quality, green tea tea bags
30g (1oz) salted butter
½ tsp ground Sichuan pepper or white pepper
1 tbsp chives, finely chopped

for the salsa
2 baby cucumbers, deseeded and finely diced
12 salad radishes, finely sliced
a pinch of salt
2 tbsp konbu sushi vinegar (see page 47)

Remove the heads and shells of the prawns. Make shallow slits along their backs to remove the black vein but leave the tails on.

Bring the water to the boil in a frying pan and let the tea bags steep for 5 minutes. Remove the bags. Turn the heat down low, keeping the water at a gently rolling boil, and cook the prawns for 3–5 minutes, so that they cook through and take on the flavour of the green tea.

Carefully pour away all but 2 tablespoons of the tea and add the butter. Increase the heat until the butter begins to sizzle, then remove from the heat and add the pepper and chopped chives.

In a small mixing bowl combine the cucumbers, radishes, salt and sushi vinegar.

Give each person 5 prawns and serve with the cucumber salsa.

salmon teriyaki with garlic baby potatoes

A very popular item at YO! Sushi, this is an irresistible combination of succulent, fresh salmon and teriyaki sauce. Teriyaki sauce goes with practically any fish or meat but especially well with oily fish such as salmon, mackerel or tuna.

serves 4

4 salmon fillets, each weighing 100g (3½oz)
1 tbsp vegetable oil
½ tsp sea salt
4 tbsp teriyaki sauce (see page 40)

for the potatoes
500g (1lb 2oz) baby potatoes, cleaned
2 tbsp extra virgin olive oil
zest and juice of ½ lemon,
1 garlic clove, peeled and crushed
1 tbsp capers, drained
50g (2oz) wild rocket, roughly torn
salt and ground black pepper

Preheat the grill to high and line the grill pan with foil.

Put the potatoes in a saucepan of cold water and bring to the boil, cooking them for 10 minutes or until they are tender. Drain.

While the potatoes are boiling, cook the salmon. Brush the fillets with the oil and sprinkle with the salt, then place skin-side down under the grill and cook for 5 minutes. Turn them over and cook for a further 3 minutes or until the skin becomes slightly blistered.

Reduce the heat to medium and brush the fish with the teriyaki sauce. Put the fish back under the grill for 1–2 minutes, then brush on more teriyaki sauce. Repeat this process twice, reserving a small amount of teriyaki sauce to brush on just before serving.

Put the potatoes in a large bowl and break them up roughly with a fork. Drizzle over the olive oil and add the lemon juice and zest, crushed garlic and capers. Fold in the rocket leaves and adjust the seasoning with salt and pepper.

Place a piece of salmon on each plate, brush with the reserved teriyaki sauce and serve with the potatoes.

sake-marinated sole with steamed pak choi

This is a fast, simple and fail-safe way of cooking any delicately flavoured white fish, such as sole. A wonderful aroma emerges as the impressive-looking parcels are opened at the table.

serves 4

4 sole fillets, each weighing 100g (3^1/$_2$oz)
^{1}/$_2$ tsp sea salt
4 tbsp sake
4 tsp vegetable oil
4 heads pak choi, cleaned and cut in half lengthways
4 slices lemon or lime
4 fresh shiitake mushrooms (caps only – discard the stems)

4 sheets of baking parchment or foil, 30cm x 30cm (12in x 12in)

Place the sole fillets on a large plate, sprinkle with salt and sake and set aside for 20 minutes. Do not to pour away the sake when the fish has finished marinating. Preheat the oven to 190°C/375°F/gas mark 5.

Lightly brush the paper or foil with the oil. Place 2 pieces of pak choi in the middle of each square and lay one fillet on top. Put a slice of lemon and a shiitake mushroom on top of the fish and drizzle over the reserved sake marinade. Gather together the edges of the paper or foil and seal tightly to make a parcel. Repeat this process for each piece of fish. Place the 4 parcels on a baking tray and cook in the oven for 10 minutes. Serve the parcels on warm plates, letting your guests open them.

sesame salmon with leeks and shiitake mushrooms

Steaming is a very gentle and forgiving way of cooking that is particularly suited to fish and vegetables. In this recipe the salmon is infused with the subtle aroma of toasted sesame oil. It is best served with hot, plain boiled rice to mop up all the juices. You will need a medium-size steamer saucepan or some bamboo steaming baskets.

serves 4

4 salmon fillets, each weighing 175g (6oz)
4 tbsp sake
3 tbsp soy sauce
1 tsp juice from grated fresh root ginger
1 tsp toasted sesame oil
4 fresh shiitake mushrooms, stalks removed
  and discarded
1 medium leek, cut into in 1.5cm (¾in) slices
2 tbsp cornflour, dissolved in 4 tbsp water
1 tbsp cress, to garnish
1 tsp toasted sesame seeds, to garnish

Cut the salmon fillets into 2cm x 2cm (¾in x (¾in) cubes and place them in a bowl that will fit inside your steamer. Add the sake, soy sauce, ginger juice and sesame oil and gently stir to coat the salmon pieces.

Cut the shiitake mushroom caps in half, then add them and the sliced leek to the salmon. Pour over the cornflour and stir gently.

Cover the bowl with foil and place in the steamer for 18–20 minutes. Divide among 4 warm dishes, garnish with the cress and sesame seeds, and serve.

YO! Sushi tip
Try this recipe with a firm white fish such as sea bass or haddock.

duck breast with soba noodles and spinach

The richness of duck combines perfectly with the nutty flavour of soba noodles. The key to getting duck really crispy is in keeping the skin dry before cooking.

serves 4

4 duck breasts
2 tsp salt

for the soba noodle salad
400g (14oz) dry soba noodles
2 tsp toasted sesame oil
80g (3¼oz) baby spinach leaves, washed
    and drained
100ml (3½fl oz) ponzu dressing (see page 47)

Bring a large saucepan of water to just below boiling and leave to simmer while you attend to the duck.

Trim off any excess fat from the duck breasts and prick the skin with a fork. Rub ½ teaspoon of salt into each breast, skin-side only. Put a non-stick frying pan over a medium to high heat and pat the breasts dry with kitchen paper before placing them skin-side down in the pan for 5–6 minutes (no cooking oil is required as the duck cooks in its own fat). Remove the duck from the pan and discard the fat.

Reheat the pan over a high heat, and when it is very hot, put the duck breasts back into the pan, skin-side up, and cook for 2 minutes to seal. Turn the duck over and cook it skin-side down for 4–5 minutes, or until it is crisp and golden. Transfer the duck to a plate, cover lightly with foil and leave to rest while you cook the soba noodles.

Increase the heat under the saucepan of water to bring it to a rolling boil and add the noodles. Stir gently to separate the strands. Stand by with a glass of cold water and pour it in when the cooking water rises to the surface (see page 22 for advice on cooking noodles). Bring the water back to the boil and cook for 2–3 minutes before draining the noodles in a large colander. Rinse the noodles under cold running water and drain well, then drizzle over the toasted sesame oil. Add the spinach, folding it into the noodles.

Carve the duck breasts into slices 5mm (¼in) thick. Divide the noodle salad among 4 plates and arrange the duck slices on the top. Drizzle the ponzu dressing over the top and serve immediately.

chicken teriyaki with green beans and baby corn

Chicken in teriyaki sauce is a classic Japanese combination. To bring out the best in both ingredients, pre-cook the chicken before basting it with the sauce so that the teriyaki sauce does not burn and become bitter. It is best to use boneless chicken thighs rather than breasts as they are more succulent.

serves 4

8 boneless chicken thighs
½ tsp salt
125ml (4½fl oz) teriyaki sauce (see page 40)
1 handful of fine beans, trimmed
1 handful of baby corn cobs, cut in half lengthways
½ tsp shichimi togarashi (Japanese seven-spice chilli powder)

Preheat the grill to high. Line the grill pan with foil to catch drips and place it with the rack under the grill to preheat (preheating the rack will stop the chicken sticking to it).

Prick the chicken thighs with a fork and sprinkle the salt over the skin. Lay the chicken skin-side up on the rack and grill for 5 minutes, then turn it over to cook on the other side for 3 minutes. To test that the chicken is cooked, pierce the thickest part of the thighs with a sharp knife. The juices should run clear.

Set aside 2 tablespoons of the teriyaki sauce. Brush both sides of the chicken with the remaining teriyaki sauce and return to the grill for 1 minute. Brush with teriyaki sauce once more, taking care not to let the teriyaki sauce burn. While the chicken is cooking, steam the beans and corn for 2–3 minutes.

Arrange 2 chicken thighs, some beans and corn cobs on each plate and sprinkle with the shichimi togarashi. Drizzle the 2 tablespoons of reserved teriyaki sauce over the chicken and vegetables. Serve immediately.

YO! Sushi tip
If you prefer to use chicken breasts, keep the skin on and brush them with a small amount of vegetable oil to keep them moist.

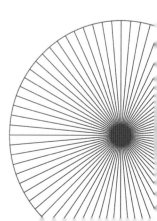

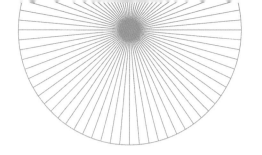

japanese chicken with pumpkin

The addition of a little rice vinegar to teriyaki sauce gives it a sweet-and-sour flavour. The sauce marries well with the sweetness of pumpkin and makes the whole dish satisfying and very comforting. You will need a non-stick frying pan with a well-fitting lid.

serves 4

8 boneless chicken thighs
2 tbsp cornflour, sifted, for dusting
400g (14oz) pumpkin or butternut squash,
   peeled and seeds removed
300ml (10fl oz) water
1 tbsp mirin or sugar
a pinch of salt
2 tbsp vegetable oil
100ml (3½fl oz) sake
100ml (3½fl oz) teriyaki sauce (see page 40)
2 tsp ginger juice, squeezed from grated
   fresh root ginger
4 tbsp rice vinegar

Place the chicken thighs skin-side down on a chopping board and make some shallow incisions, taking care not to cut all the way through. Dust with sifted cornflour.

Cut the pumpkin into wedges 2.5cm (1in) thick. Put them in a large saucepan with the water, mirin or sugar and the salt, and bring to the boil over a medium heat. Reduce the heat to low once the water begins to boil, cover with a lid and simmer for 12–15 minutes.

While the pumpkin simmers, cook the chicken thighs. Heat a non-stick frying pan over a high heat and add the oil. Cook the chicken skin-side down for 3 minutes, then reduce the heat. Turn the chicken over and cook it on the other side for 2 minutes. Cover with a lid and allow to steam for a further 3 minutes.

Remove the lid and add the sake, teriyaki sauce and ginger juice, shaking the pan gently to distribute the sauce evenly. When the cooking juices begin to thicken, add the rice vinegar and stir well. Turn off the heat, remove the chicken with a slotted spoon and cut into bite-size pieces. Cover with foil to keep warm and reserve the juices in the pan. Drain the pumpkin wedges.

Arrange the chicken and pumpkin in 4 warm dishes, drizzle over the chicken cooking juices and serve.

YO! Sushi tip
Try using boneless duck thighs.

japanese beef steak with wasabi garlic butter

The *Wagyu,* or Japanese beef cattle, of Kobe are incredibly well looked after. They are hand fed on a special high-protein diet, given beer and sake to tenderise the meat, their bodies massaged to disperse the fat and kept in clean air-conditioned sheds. It is no wonder that Kobe beef is internationally recognised for its beautiful, marbled meat. The meat is very rich, so one would want to eat only a small amount – just as well, because it is very expensive. Of course for this recipe it is perfectly acceptable to use high-quality sirloin.

serves 4

100g (3½oz) salted butter, softened but not melting
4 tsp wasabi paste
1 garlic clove, peeled and crushed
4 top-quality sirloin steaks, each weighing 200g
   (7oz), at room temperature
1 tsp toasted sesame oil
salt and ground black pepper
2 tbsp soy sauce
1 tbsp finely chopped chives

Mix the softened butter with the wasabi paste and crushed garlic and transfer to a piece of cling film. Wrap the butter mixture in the cling film and roll it into a small log 3cm (1¼in) in diameter. Refrigerate the butter for 15–20 minutes or until firm.

Heat a heavy-based, non-stick frying pan over a medium heat. Brush the steaks with the sesame oil and season with salt and pepper. Turn up the heat to high and cook the steaks for 3–5 minutes on each side for medium rare or 5–7 minutes if you prefer them well-done. Remove the steaks from the pan, cover them with foil and leave them to rest on warm plates for 5 minutes. Reduce the heat and add the soy sauce to the pan, stirring well. Take the butter out of the refrigerator, remove the cling film and cut it into 8 slices. Spoon the cooking juices over the steaks, top with a couple of slices of butter and sprinkle with the finely chopped chives. Serve immediately.

YO! Sushi tip
This is wonderful served with boiled new potatoes and steamed Chinese broccoli or tenderstem broccoli.

niku jaga (simmered beef with potatoes)

In this recipe, three most un-Japanese ingredients combine to make one of Japan's most quintessential examples of home cooking. Each family has its own recipe, which is passed on from mother to daughter.

serves 4

400g (14oz) potatoes, peeled and cut
  into large chunks
400ml (14fl oz) dashi stock (see page 16)
1 onion, peeled and cut into 8 wedges
3 tbsp sugar
2 tbsp sake
4 tbsp soy sauce
300g (10oz) topside or silverside beef, thinly sliced
salt (optional)
50g (2oz) mangetout, trimmed and blanched in
  boiling water for 30 seconds

Put the potatoes in a large saucepan, adding enough water to cover them, and bring to the boil over a medium heat. Once the water begins to boil, reduce the heat, simmer for 10–12 minutes, then drain.

Put the parboiled potatoes back into the saucepan with the dashi stock, add the onion and bring to the boil over a medium heat. Once the stock is boiling, reduce the heat to low, add the sugar and simmer for 5 minutes. Add the sake and soy sauce and simmer for 10 minutes more before adding the beef. Simmer for 4–5 minutes while spooning off any scum that floats to the surface. Season with salt if necessary, then remove from the heat, add the mangetout, transfer to a large serving bowl and serve.

YO! Sushi tip
If you want to make the dish more substantial, add either prepared glass noodles or cooked udon noodles towards the end of cooking.

firecracker rice

Fried rice is a quick and delicious way to use up leftover cooked rice and whatever vegetables you find in your refrigerator. Do remember that it works much better with cold rice, so if you are making this dish fresh, be sure to let the rice cool down before you fry it.

serves 4

3 tbsp vegetable oil
1 onion, finely chopped
1 carrot, peeled and finely diced
1 red pepper, deseeded and diced
1 yellow pepper, deseeded and diced
2 garlic cloves, crushed
4 tbsp frozen edamame, cooked for 5 minutes and shelled, or 4 tbsp cooked green peas
1 tsp toasted sesame oil
600g (1¼lb) cold cooked rice (see pages 18–19)
4 tbsp light soy sauce
½ tsp freshly ground white pepper
½ tsp shichimi togarashi (Japanese seven-spice chilli powder)
4 tsp spring onion, finely chopped, to garnish

Heat a large wok or non-stick frying pan over a medium heat and add 2 tablespoons of vegetable oil. Allow the oil to heat up before adding the chopped onion. Stir-fry for 2–3 minutes then add the carrot, red and yellow pepper, garlic and edamame. Cook for 3 minutes, then remove the vegetables with a slotted spoon and set aside.

Add the remaining vegetable oil, if required, together with the sesame oil. Add the rice, separating the grains with a wooden spatula so that there are no large lumps, and stir-fry for 2–3 minutes. Return the vegetables to the pan, tossing and stirring to mix them thoroughly with the rice. Pour the soy sauce along the edge of the wok or pan, season with the white pepper and shichimi togarashi and stir to mix well.

Remove from the heat, divide the rice into 4 equal portions, garnish with the chopped spring onion and serve.

YO! Sushi tip
It's best to use light soy sauce so as not to discolour the vegetables and rice. If you only have the dark variety, you may need to add a pinch of salt.

mushroom rice

Italians celebrate autumn with white truffles whereas the Japanese feast on the most prized and uniquely fragrant matsutake mushroom. A homegrown matsutake weighing 40g (1½oz) fetches an eye-popping £100 at the beginning of October. But don't worry, this recipe calls not for matsutake but for Japanese mushrooms like shimeji and enoki, which are becoming easier and easier to find on supermarket shelves. If you can't find these, use shiitake and oyster mushrooms.

serves 4

400g (14oz) rice (see pages 18–19)
8 caps dried shiitake mushrooms
300g (10oz) fresh Japanese mushrooms,
   e.g. shiitake, shimeji, enoki, maitake
400ml (14fl oz) warm water
4 tbsp sake
2 tbsp mirin
4 tbsp soy sauce
½ tsp salt
1 tsp toasted sesame seeds, to garnish

Start by washing the rice as described on page 18. Leave the washed rice in a sieve to drain for at least 30 minutes (preferably 1 hour). Meanwhile, soak the dried shiitake mushrooms in the warm water until soft, remove once the water has cooled down. Gently squeeze the mushrooms to remove the moisture, reserving the soaking liquid, then discard the stalks and slice the caps.

Remove and discard the stalks of the fresh shiitake mushrooms and slice the caps. For shimeji, enoki and maitake, cut off and discard the bases. Put all the fresh mushrooms in a bowl add the sake, mirin, soy sauce and salt. Leave to soak for 10 minutes.

Put all the ingredients, including the reserved shiitake liquor and the rice, in a large heavy-based saucepan with a tight-fitting lid and bring to a gentle rolling boil over a medium heat. Resist the temptation to lift the lid to take a look; instead, listen out for bubbling sounds that will tell you the rice is boiling. Turn the heat up to high when you hear it start to boil, cook for 3 minutes, then remove from the heat. Leave it to steam for 10 minutes – do not lift the lid until it has finished steaming.

Stir the rice with a flat wooden spatula in cut-and-turn motions and serve warm, garnished with the sesame seeds.

green pea rice

Fresh peas in the pod have an almost intense sweetness. Although it is tempting to add other vegetables, cooking them alone brings out their pure taste. Serve with a bowl of miso soup with clams (see page 63).

serves 4

400g (14oz) rice (see pages 18–19)
500g (1lb 2oz) fresh peas in the pod
480ml (17fl oz) water
1½ tsp salt
1½ tbsp mirin

Rinse the rice until the water runs clear and set aside in a sieve for 30 minutes. Shell the peas just before you want to start cooking and quickly wash them.

Put all the ingredients in a heavy-based saucepan with a tight-fitting lid and bring to the boil over a low to medium heat. Do not lift the lid to see whether it has reached boiling point but listen out for bubbling sounds and signs of steam. Once it has boiled, turn up the heat and cook for 3–4 minutes, then remove from the heat. Do not lift the lid but let the rice steam for 10 minutes. Fluff up and serve.

YO! Sushi tip
Try this recipe with edamame: cook them in their shells in lightly salted water, then remove the thin inner skin.

roasted red pepper stuffed sushi

Inari zushi, or 'stuffed sushi', are traditionally made using seasoned deep-fried tofu pouches to enclose the stuffing. They are sold ready to use in Japanese grocery stores. This recipe calls for peppers instead of tofu – they are easy to prepare and equally tasty.

serves 4 as a starter, 2 as a main course

4 red peppers
1 tbsp vegetable oil, for brushing
200g (7oz) prepared sushi rice (see pages 19–21)
1 tbsp toasted sesame seeds
4 sprigs of flat-leaf parsley, to garnish

Preheat the oven to 180°C/350°F/gas mark 4. Line a roasting tray with a piece of foil and place in the oven to heat. Cut the peppers in half lengthways, discarding the seeds, and brush them inside and out with the oil. Put on the hot roasting tray and cook for 12–15 minutes or until they have begun to soften but still retain their shape. Mix the sushi rice with the sesame seeds.

Take the peppers out of the oven and let them cool down enough to handle. Scoop out any cooking juice and discard.

Divide the sushi rice mixture into 8 equal egg-shaped portions and place in the roasted pepper half. Garnish with the parsley and serve.

crab somen noodles

This dish is a real winner on hot summer days. If using frozen crabmeat, defrost thoroughly before using.

serves 4

200g (7oz) dry somen noodles
1 red onion, thinly sliced and soaked in cold water
200g (7oz) cooked white crabmeat
2 tsp grated fresh root ginger
2 tbsp light soy sauce
1 tbsp yuzu juice or lime juice
4 tsp cress, to garnish

Bring a large saucepan of water to the boil and cook the somen noodles as described on page 22. Rinse the noodles in ice-cold water and set aside in a colander to drain well. Drain the soaked onion.

Put the noodles, onion, crabmeat and the remaining ingredients in a bowl and gently mix.

Divide into 4 equal portions, garnish with the cress and serve.

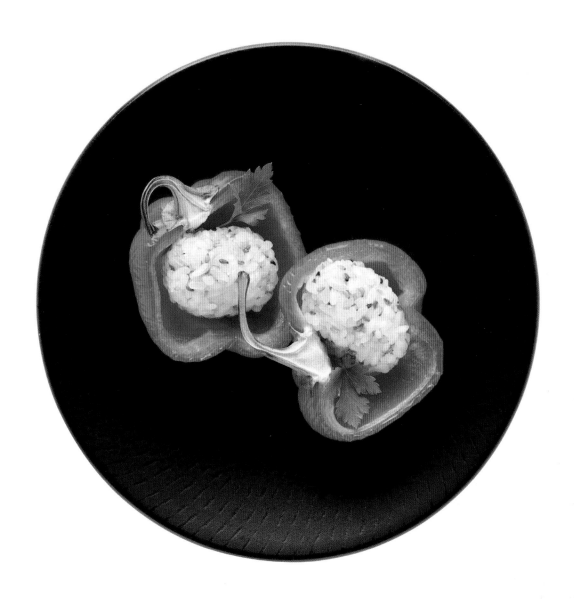

gravadlax sushi balls

Sushi balls, or *temari zushi,* are deceptively easy to make, impressive to look at and utterly delicious. They make an irresistible canapé or stylish starter and you don't need any special equipment – just some cling film.

makes about 20 balls

dash of vinegar
60g (2¹/₄oz) gravadlax or smoked salmon, cut into
    20 squares the size of postage stamps
300g (10oz) prepared sushi rice (see pages 19–21)
1 tsp wasabi paste, to serve
soy sauce, to serve

Add a dash of vinegar to a small bowl of cold water and have the water and a dessertspoon ready. Lay a piece of cling film, 10cm x 10cm (4in x 4in) square, on a clean work surface. Place a piece of gravadlax in the centre of the cling film. Wet the spoon in the bowl of water and take a heaped spoonful of the prepared sushi rice. Place the rice on top of the piece of gravadlax and shape it into a small mound with your fingers. Pick up all 4 corners of the cling film, gathering them over the rice, and twist the cling film to shape the rice mound into a ball. Unwrap the cling film and set the ball down on a plate with the gravadlax on top. Cover it gently with a clean, damp tea towel while you make more balls.

Arrange the sushi balls on a plate and serve with the wasabi paste and a dish of soy sauce for dipping.

YO! Sushi tip
Try making this with cooked prawns.

mushroom and egg chirashi sushi

Chirashi means 'scattered'. Chirashi sushi is the easiest sushi to make and can be varied infinitely, so feel free to incorporate whatever is in season to suit your taste and mood. Always remember that good sushi begins with good sushi rice – so follow the section on how to prepare sushi rice on pages 19–21.

serves 4

1 tbsp butter
4 medium eggs, lightly beaten
1 tbsp mirin
1 tbsp vegetable oil
200g (7oz) fresh Japanese mushrooms of your
   choice, e.g. shimeji or enoki, roughly chopped
1 tbsp light soy sauce
1 tbsp sushi vinegar
600g (1¼lb) prepared sushi rice (see pages 19–21)
2 tbsp toasted sesame seeds, to garnish

Melt the butter in an omelette pan or small frying pan placed over a medium heat. Mix the eggs and mirin in a bowl and add to the pan. When the egg mixture starts to set, stir vigorously with 2 chopsticks or a whisk. Remove the scrambled egg from the pan and set aside. Heat the oil in the pan and cook the mushrooms for 2–3 minutes or until they begin to wilt. Season with the soy sauce.

Drizzle the sushi vinegar into a large non-metallic mixing bowl and swirl to moisten the inside – this will stop the rice sticking. Put the prepared sushi rice in the bowl and fold in the scrambled egg and mushrooms.

Arrange the sushi mixture on 4 dishes, sprinkle over the sesame seeds and serve.

YO! Sushi tip
In spring, try this with steamed asparagus and scrambled egg; in summer, cooked peas and raw vine tomatoes are delicious. For those who like a bit of a kick to their food, try crabmeat, lime and fresh chilli.

fresh fruit yakitori with strawberry dipping sauce

There is no equivalent of dessert in the traditional Japanese meal but a few slices of seasonal fruit may be served at the end of a meal. There are, however, many traditional Japanese sweets and cakes, which are served as mid-afternoon snacks with Japanese green tea. While it may not be traditional to round off a Japanese meal with something sweet, it is certainly enjoyable.

This simple dish combines seasonal fruits with traditional Japanese seasoning.

serves 4

8 bamboo skewers, soaked in water for 30 minutes
1 slightly under-ripe fresh mango
2 slightly under-ripe fresh peaches
200g (7oz) fresh pineapple, cut into bite-size
    chunks
2 tbsp mirin
1 tbsp demerara sugar, for sprinkling

for the strawberry dipping sauce
125g (4½oz) strawberries, hulled
25g (1oz) caster sugar
1 tsp balsamic vinegar
pinch of freshly ground black pepper

To make the strawberry dipping sauce, put all the ingredients in a food processor or blender and purée until smooth. Put to one side while you make the fruit yakitori.

Preheat the grill to high. Line the grill pan with foil, put the rack on top and place under the grill to heat up. Meanwhile, cut a slice off the mango along the edge of the stone. Repeat the other side. Score the flesh in each half into 4 pieces, then push the skin side of the mango until the cubes stick out. Cut the cubes off with a knife. Remove the stones from the peaches and cut into bite-size pieces.

Slide the pineapple, peach and mango pieces onto each soaked bamboo skewer, alternating between the different fruits. Lay the skewers on the grill rack, brush with the mirin and sprinkle over the sugar. Grill for 2–3 minutes on each side or until the sugar has melted and is about to caramelise. Serve immediately with the sauce on the side

green tea ice cream

The slight bitterness of the matcha (the fine green tea powder used in tea ceremonies) complements the sweetness of the vanilla ice cream and adds a sophisticated touch. Matcha is sold in small tins – it is expensive but a little goes a long way. Store in the refrigerator and use within six months.

serves 4

500ml (18fl oz) top-quality vanilla ice cream
1 tbsp matcha (green tea powder)
1 tbsp tepid water

Take the ice cream out of the freezer and let it stand at room temperature for 10–15 minutes to soften – but do not let it melt. In a large mixing bowl, combine the matcha with the tepid water to make a smooth paste. Add half the ice cream and mix well before adding the remainder. Mix again until is becomes marbled or, if you prefer, continue until it becomes evenly coloured. Return the ice-cream to its carton.

Put the ice cream back into the freezer for 30–45 minutes to firm up before serving.

very berry

This is a fruit salad with a distinctive Japanese twist: the addition of yuzu juice, which has a refreshing citrus flavour.

serves 4

100g (3½oz) sugar
125ml (4½fl oz) water
2 tsp yuzu juice
200g (7oz) strawberries
100g (3½oz) blueberries
100g (3½oz) blackberries
100g (3½oz) raspberries
a few sprigs of fresh mint, to decorate

Mix the sugar and water in a heavy-based saucepan over a high heat and stir to dissolve the sugar. Allow the sugar water to boil and reduce in volume until it has thickened and become syrupy. Set the syrup aside to cool then add the yuzu juice.

Meanwhile, wash and drain the fruit and remove any stalks. Put the fruit in a large, glass serving bowl, drizzle with the syrup and stir gently. Decorate with the mint and serve.

This recipe is inspired by a Swiss dessert called Mont Blanc. This Japanese version is as delicious as the mountain is awe-inspiring.

serves 4

2 egg whites
1 tbsp caster sugar
200ml (7fl oz) mascarpone cheese
    or soft cream cheese
4 tbsp ready-made adzuki bean jam, plus 4 tsp
    for decorating
4 ready-made meringue nests
icing sugar, for dusting

Whisk the egg whites until stiff peaks form, then gently sprinkle over the sugar and fold it in. Little by little, spoon in the mascarpone and fold in gently.

Place a spoonful of adzuki bean jam in the middle of each meringue nest and top with the egg and mascarpone mixture. Dust with the icing sugar, top with a little more adzuki bean jam and serve.

apprentice
get rolling with these everyday recipes

three
gyoza

Gyoza are delectable fried dumplings filled with minced vegetables, chicken or prawns. Originating in China, gyoza are very popular in Japan. The fillings are encased in gyoza skins, which are sold frozen in packs of 20 in Asian food stores.

serves 4

20–25 gyoza skins
1 tbsp vegetable oil, for cooking
gyoza dipping sauce, to serve (see page 41)

for the vegetable filling
4 dried shiitake mushrooms, softened in warm water
    for 10 minutes and the soaking liquor reserved
    stems discarded and caps finely chopped
1 onion, finely chopped
1 carrot, peeled and finely chopped
1 leek, trimmed and finely chopped
4 leaves Savoy cabbage, finely chopped
1 garlic clove, crushed
½ tbsp grated fresh root ginger
1 tsp toasted sesame oil
1 heaped tbsp cornflour

for the chicken filling
2 dried shiitake mushrooms, prepared as above
200g (7oz) minced chicken
½ leek, trimmed and finely chopped
1 garlic clove, crushed
1 tsp grated fresh root ginger
1 tsp toasted sesame oil
1 tbsp cornflour

for the prawn filling
200g (7oz) cooked shelled prawns, well drained
1 onion, finely chopped
2 tbsp coriander, finely chopped
1 tsp grated fresh root ginger
1 tbsp cornflour

For each filling, put all the listed ingredients in a bowl and mix well. Take a gyoza skin in one hand. With a pastry brush, moisten the top half of the skin with water (if making vegetable gyoza, use the mushroom soaking liquor). Put a large teaspoonful of filling in the centre. Fold the lower half of the skin over the filling, edge to edge, pressing down to stick the 2 edges together. The fillings will make about 20 dumplings.

Heat a large frying pan over a medium heat and add the oil. Lay half the gyoza flat-side down in the frying pan and cook for 3–5 minutes or until the underside is browned and crisp. Turn the gyoza over with a pair of tongs or chopsticks and cook the other side for 3 minutes. Remove from the pan and keep warm. Cook the remaining gyoza in the same way, then return all the gyoza to the pan. Pour in half a glass of water and immediately cover the pan with a lid. Steam the gyoza until the water has gone.

Allow 5 gyoza per person and serve with a dish of gyoza dipping sauce.

YO! Sushi tip
Gyoza skins can be refrozen if you have some left over. Make a large batch of gyoza and freeze them uncooked. Frozen gyoza should be cooked as described above but a full cup of water will be needed for steaming them.

pumpkin korroke

This is a fine example of Japanese home cooking – the sweetness of the pumpkin contrasts well with the tangy katsu sauce. Make the korroke (croquettes) in small bite-size balls to serve as a tasty canapé.

serves 4

300g (10oz) pumpkin, peeled and deseeded
1 onion, peeled and finely chopped
1 tsp vegetable oil
1 tbsp butter
1 tbsp parsley, finely chopped
½ tsp salt
¼ tsp grated nutmeg
100g (3½oz) plain flour
2 eggs, lightly beaten with 2 tbsp water
100g (3½oz) Japanese panko (or dried breadcrumbs)
vegetable oil, for frying
katsu sauce (see page 44), to serve

Chop the pumpkin flesh into 2.5cm (1in)-square chunks. Steam for 10–12 minutes or until it is soft enough to mash.

Meanwhile, sweat the chopped onion in the oil over a medium heat, being sure not to let it burn. Put the steamed pumpkin into a mixing bowl, add the butter and, with a potato masher, mash until smooth. Add the onion to the pumpkin mash. Sprinkle the chopped parsley over the top, season the pumpkin with the salt and nutmeg and mix well.

Using your hands, form the pumpkin mash into egg-size balls. Dust the balls with the flour, dip them in the egg mixture and coat with the panko.

Heat the oil in a frying pan and fry the pumpkin balls for 3–5 minutes over a medium heat or until the outside is crispy and golden. Cook them in small batches and turn them over frequently to ensure they cook all over. Using a slotted spoon, turn the balls out onto kitchen paper while you cook the others. Serve with katsu sauce.

YO! Sushi tip
Panko is sold ready made in Japanese grocery stores. Try adding 100g (3½oz) cooked chicken or beef mince for a more substantial dish.

seared scallops with wasabi miso

This recipe makes an elegant starter, especially when the scallops are served in their half-shells. Allow one large, plump scallop per person. Ask the fishmonger to prepare the scallops for you and to give you the shells.

2 tbsp dried wakame
4 scallops on the shell, trimmed and the
    coral removed
1 tbsp vegetable oil
½ tsp toasted sesame oil
salt and ground white pepper
1 tbsp rice vinegar
1 tsp soy sauce
½ tsp sake or rice vinegar
2 tsp ikura (salmon roe)

for the wasabi miso
1 tbsp light-coloured miso paste
1 tsp wasabi
1 tbsp mirin

Start by soaking the wakame in a bowl of tepid water for 10 minutes. Meanwhile, scrub the outside of the scallop shells. Clean the inside of the shells and wipe dry with kitchen paper. Slice the scallops in half.

Heat a heavy cast-iron griddle over a medium heat. While it is heating, mix the vegetable and sesame oils together and brush over the scallops, then season them with salt and pepper. When the griddle is very hot, sear the scallops for 1 minute on each side.

Drain the softened wakame and mix it with the rice vinegar and soy sauce, then divide the wakame among the 4 cleaned scallop shells. In a bowl, add the sake or rice vinegar to the ikura to separate the eggs.

To make the wasabi miso, mix all the ingredients in a small bowl.

Put 2 scallop halves on top of each pile of wakame and spoon over the wasabi miso, then top with half a teaspoon of ikura. Place a scallop shell on top and serve.

seared tuna salad

Searing the tuna seals in the flavour of the fish and gives you wonderfully contrasting textures. The key to success is not to overcook it.

serves 4

4 tuna steaks, each weighing 100g (3½oz)
1 tbsp vegetable oil
salt and ground black pepper
½ white or red onion, peeled and thinly sliced
4 tbsp rice vinegar
100g (3½oz) watercress
100g (3½oz) baby spinach leaves
40g (1½oz) daikon (giant white Japanese radish), finely shredded
10g (½oz) fresh root ginger, peeled and thinly sliced
125ml (4½fl oz) ponzu dressing (see page 47)
1 tsp toasted sesame seeds

Preheat a heavy, cast-iron griddle until very hot. Brush the tuna steaks with the oil and season with salt and pepper. Meanwhile, soak the sliced onion in a bowl of cold water for 10 minutes – this takes away the oniony smell and refreshes it. Put the tuna steaks onto the griddle and sear on one side for 1 minute, then turn them over and cook the other side for just under 1 minute. Remove the steaks to a plate, drizzle with the rice vinegar and set aside to rest.

Drain the onion slices. Put the watercress, spinach, daikon and ginger in a bowl and dress with the ponzu. Divide the salad among 4 individual serving plates and sprinkle with the sesame seeds. Slice the tuna steaks into thick, bite-size chunks, arrange on top of the salad and serve.

YO! Sushi tip
If you can't get daikon, use ordinary salad radishes instead.

warm beetroot salad with sweet soy vinegar

This vibrant salad makes a perfect starter or side dish.

serves 4

2 fresh beetroot, the size of a tennis ball
2 spring onions, finely chopped
2 tbsp bonito flakes
1 tsp toasted sesame seeds

for the sweet soy vinegar
4 tbsp rice vinegar
1 tbsp sugar
1 tsp light soy sauce
1 tbsp mirin

Cut the leaves off the beetroot and discard. Boil the beetroot for 20–25 minutes, then remove them from the water and set aside until they are cool enough to handle.

While they are cooling, combine all the ingredients for the sweet soy vinegar in a heat-resistant glass bowl and microwave at a medium heat for 30 seconds to warm through (or in a small saucepan for 1 minute).

Peel the beetroot with a potato peeler and trim the top and roots. Cut the beetroot in half and then into thin, half-moon slices.

Arrange the sliced beetroot on warm plates, allowing half a beetroot per person. Drizzle with the warm vinegar mixture and top with the spring onion and bonito flakes. Sprinkle over the sesame seeds and serve warm.

agedashi tofu

This is a typical Zen Buddhist vegetarian dish, but you don't need to be a Buddhist to enjoy this subtle yet satisfying way to eat tofu.

serves 4

2 blocks silken tofu, each weighing 300g (10oz)
vegetable oil, for deep-frying
4 tbsp plain flour
2 tsp grated fresh root ginger, to garnish
1 spring onion, finely sliced, to garnish

for the dashi broth
300ml (10fl oz) vegetarian dashi stock
   (see page 17)
4 tbsp light soy sauce
4 tbsp mirin

First of all, drain the tofu by wrapping it in 2 sheets of kitchen paper and letting it stand for 15–20 minutes.

Put all the ingredients for the dashi broth in a saucepan and gently heat, being sure not to let the broth boil. Turn down the heat and keep warm.

Put the oil in a heavy-based, deep frying pan and heat to about 180°C/350°F. Test the oil temperature by dropping in a small piece of tofu. The tofu will sink to the bottom of the pan before floating back to the surface if the temperature is too low, or will not sink at all if the temperature is too high. At the right temperature the tofu should sink halfway down, then float back to the surface.

Cut each tofu block in half and dust with the flour, then gently slide the tofu into the oil and deep-fry until the outside turns crisp and golden. Arrange the cooked tofu on 4 warm serving dishes, gently ladle some dashi broth to one side of the tofu and garnish with the grated ginger and sliced spring onion. Serve immediately.

YO! Sushi tip
Go easy with the flour when you are dusting the tofu and don't dust it until you are ready to deep-fry it, otherwise it will become sticky.

japanese
rolled omelette

There is nothing difficult about making a rolled omelette – it is easier than it looks. All that is needed is a sushi rolling mat. A rectangular Japanese omelette pan does make it easier to shape but it is not essential for making this deliciously succulent omelette.

serves 4

6 large eggs, lightly beaten
40ml (1 1/2fl oz) dashi stock
1 1/2 tbsp sugar
3 tsp light soy sauce
vegetable oil, for frying

Mix the eggs, dashi stock, sugar and soy sauce in a bowl. The proportion of eggs to dashi stock is always 4:1 – in other words, you need a quarter as much dashi stock as egg by volume. The amount of sugar can be varied to taste.

Heat a non-stick frying pan over a medium heat and wipe with a piece of kitchen paper that has been soaked in oil. Pour in enough egg mixture to just cover the pan. As the egg mixture cooks and begins to bubble up, press it down with a pair of chopsticks or spatula and roll it lengthways towards you – you should have a log-shaped omelette. Move it to the end of the pan furthest away from you. Wipe the uncovered part of the pan with the oil-soaked kitchen paper and pour in more egg mixture, lifting the bottom of the rolled omelette already in the pan to allow the egg mixture to flow underneath. When the surface begins to dry, roll the whole omelette towards you with the first rolled omelette in the centre. Once again, move the entire rolled omelette to the far end of the pan. Wipe the bottom of the pan with oil and pour in more egg mixture, lifting up the omelette already in the pan. Repeat the process until all the egg mixture has been used. You should finish with a thick, log-shaped omelette.

Wrap the sushi rolling mat in a piece of cling film. Turn the rolled omelette onto the sushi mat and use the mat to mould it into a block shape.

Cut the omelette into 12 2.5cm (1in)-thick pieces, allowing 3 pieces per person. Serve warm or at room temperature.

YO! Sushi tip
As you get more confident, try layering the omelette with sheets of sushi nori. This not only creates a beautiful whirlpool effect but also adds extra flavours and nutrients.

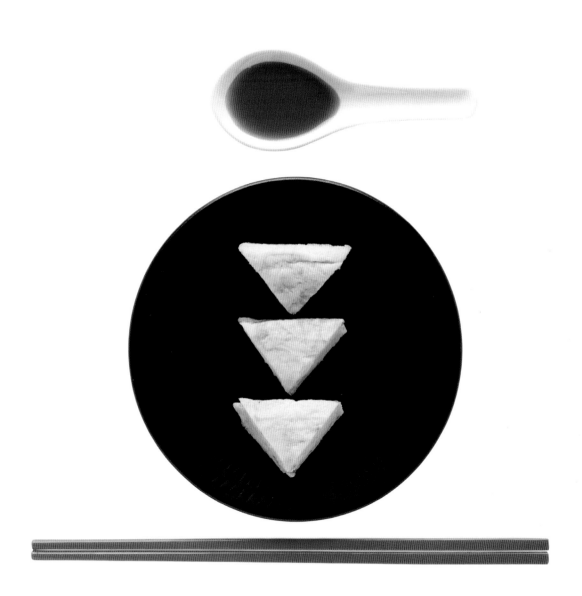

john dory salad

John Dory has delicately flavoured, firm, white meat. You may find it difficult to fillet and skin – so ask your fishmonger.

serves 4

400g (14oz) John Dory fillet, skin removed
200g (7oz) daikon salad (see page 181)
1 red onion, peeled and thinly sliced
1 baby cucumber, finely shredded
2 celery sticks, strings removed and finely sliced
1 large red chilli, deseeded and thinly sliced into
    rings, to garnish

for the marinade
4 tbsp rice vinegar
1 tbsp sugar
2 tbsp ponzu dressing (see page 47)

Slice the fish as thinly as possible. Mix all the ingredients for the marinade in a shallow dish and add the fish to marinate for 10–12 minutes.

Meanwhile, prepare the daikon as described in the daikon salad recipe on page 181. Soak the onion in a bowl of cold water for 10 minutes to remove the smell, then drain. Combine the daikon salad, onion, cucumber and celery in a bowl and divide between 4 plates.

Take the fish out of the marinade and arrange on top of the salad. Garnish the fish with the chilli rings and drizzle over the remaining marinade before serving.

YO! Sushi tip
This recipe works equally well with white fish such as lemon sole, turbot, red snapper and sea bass.

oven-baked red snapper and shiitake parcel

In Japan red snapper is considered the noblest and most auspicious of fish and no celebration is complete without it. One traditional recipe calls for a whole, handsome red snapper, soaked in sake and wrapped in beautiful, hand-made Japanese paper, tied with red or gold string. This version is much simpler but equally tasty.

serves 4

4 red snapper fillets, each weighing 100g (3½oz)
½ tbsp vegetable oil, for brushing
8 caps fresh shiitake mushrooms, stems discarded
8 stems sprouting broccoli
4 slices lime, thinly sliced
4 tbsp sake
4 tsp light soy sauce
1 tsp ginger juice, squeezed from grated
   fresh root ginger

Preheat the oven to 170°C/325°F/gas mark 3. Put each snapper fillet on a piece of foil measuring about 30cm (12in)-square and brush with the oil.

Arrange 2 shiitake mushroom caps, 2 pieces of sprouting broccoli and a slice of lime on top of each fish. Pour over the sake, soy sauce and ginger juice. Gather together the edges of the foil, seal tightly and put the parcels on a baking tray to bake for 10–12 minutes in the oven.

Place a parcel of fish on each person's plate and ask your guests to open the parcels themselves.

YO! Sushi tip
Try this recipe with other white fish such as sea bass or lemon sole.

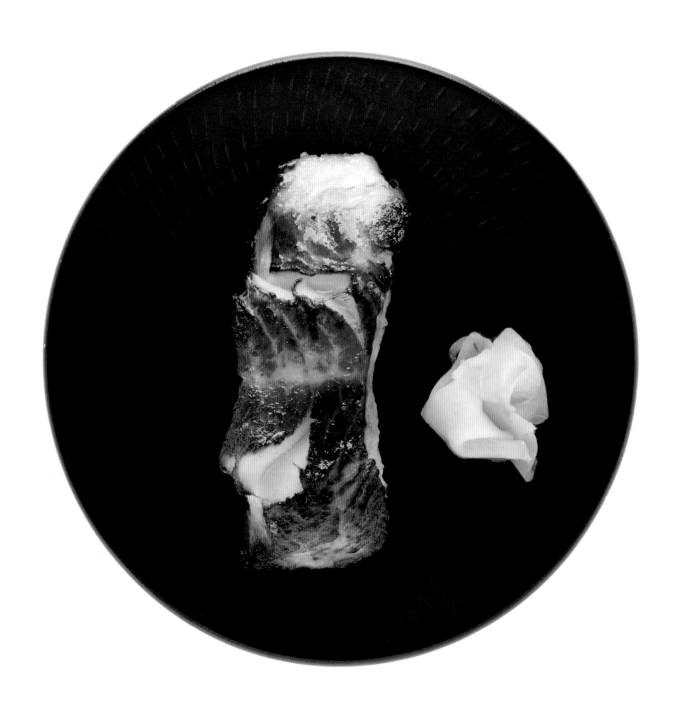

miso black cod

Black cod is one of YO! Sushi's signature dishes. 'Black cod' means two things: it can refer to a type of fish found in deep areas of the northern Pacific, as it does here, or it can be the name of a dish that uses this miso marinade with any white fish.

If you want to be authentic, you should use special light miso paste from Kyoto but this recipe has been adapted for western cooks at home. If you can't find black cod, halibut makes an excellent alternative.

serves 4

4 black cod fillets, each weighing 100g (3½oz)
4 tbsp pickled sushi ginger, to garnish

for the miso marinade
400g (14oz) light-coloured miso paste
50ml (2fl oz) mirin
2–4 tbsp sugar

First make the marinade. Mix the miso, mirin and sugar in a flat-based container with a lid. Submerge the fish in the marinade in a single layer, put the lid on and refrigerate overnight. Do not leave to marinate longer than 24 hours, as marinating it for too long will dehydrate the fish and make the taste of the miso too strong.

Preheat the grill to medium and use your hands to wipe off as much of the marinade as possible from the fish. Oil the grill rack, line the grill pan with a piece of foil and grill the fish slowly for 4–6 minutes on each side until cooked through. Watch carefully, as the sugar in the marinade makes the fish burn easily.

Serve on 4 individual serving plates, garnished with the sushi ginger.

YO! Sushi tip
The colour of miso paste provides a guide to its saltiness: the darker the colour, the saltier the miso. Authentic Saikyo miso is a pale cream and is very mild, so try to get as light a coloured miso paste as possible and adjust the amount of sugar accordingly – the lighter the miso, the less sugar you will need (see pages 12–13 for more information on miso). Try this recipe with any white fish such as sea bass or red sea bream.

grilled sushi vinegar-marinated mackerel

Mackerel is a fish rich in omega 3 that is plentiful, inexpensive and often under-rated. Marinating it in sushi vinegar before grilling makes the flesh firmer and takes away some of its fishiness.

serves 4

4 mackerel fillets, each weighing 100g (3½oz)
1½ tsp salt
12 asparagus spears, trimmed
2 tbsp soy sauce
1 lime, cut into wedges

for the sushi vinegar marinade
100ml (3½fl oz) rice vinegar
1 tbsp sugar
1½ tbsp salt

Make a few shallow slits in the skin of the mackerel and sprinkle both sides of the fish with salt. Mix all the ingredients for the sushi vinegar marinade in a large non-metallic dish, add the fish and leave to marinate for 30 minutes.

Preheat the grill to medium to high and line the grill pan with a piece of foil. Brush the asparagus with the soy sauce. Pat the mackerel dry with kitchen paper and place the fish on the centre of the grill rack, arranging the asparagus around it. Grill for 3–4 minutes on each side.

Serve each portion of fish with 3 asparagus spears and a piece of lime per person.

YO! Sushi tip
Once cooked, the fish keeps for 2–3 days. If you have any left over, try flaking it with a fork and using it in a salad.

snapper in clear broth

This is a sophisticated, delicately flavoured soup. It is important to keep the broth as clear as possible by not over-cooking it.

serves 4 as a starter

a square of konbu, 10cm x 10cm (4in x 4in)
600ml (1 pint) water
salt
150g (5oz) snapper fillet
1 tbsp sake
4 tsp cress, to garnish
1 tsp lime or lemon zest, finely sliced, to garnish

Using a pair of kitchen scissors, make some cuts in the konbu to bring out as much flavour as possible and leave it to soak in a saucepan of water for at least 30 minutes – if time allows, soak for 2 hours. Meanwhile, sprinkle a pinch of salt over the snapper and set aside for 10 to 15 minutes.

Cut the snapper into 8 small pieces. Put the pieces in a sieve and pour boiling water over them to dispel their fishy smell, then add the fish to the saucepan in which the konbu has been soaking. Heat gently, skimming off any scum that floats to the surface – be careful not to let the broth boil, as boiling will make it cloudy and spoil its delicate flavour.

Take the konbu out just before the broth reaches boiling point and season the soup with the sake and half a teaspoon of salt. Remove from the heat and gently ladle the broth and 2 pieces of fish per person into 4 warm soup bowls. Garnish with the cress and lime or lemon zest and serve.

YO! Sushi tip
You can try this recipe with other firm white fish such as John Dory, sea bream or sea bass.

chicken katsu

Chicken katsu is extremely popular in YO! Sushi restaurants. Here, the recipe has been adapted to suit home cooks and is served with refreshing sushi vinegar cucumber ribbons with ginger.

serves 4

4 skinless chicken breasts
4 tbsp plain flour, for dusting
2 eggs, lightly beaten
50g (2oz) panko (Japanese breadcrumbs or dried breadcrumbs)
125ml (4½fl oz) vegetable oil, for frying
1 lemon, cut into 4 wedges

for sushi vinegar cucumber ribbons
2 baby cucumbers
20g (¾oz) fresh root ginger, peeled and thinly sliced
2 tbsp sushi vinegar (see page 20)

Slice the chicken breasts in half horizontally – this helps them to cook quickly, so less oil is needed for frying, which is better for your health. Sift the flour onto the chicken breasts and dip them in the beaten egg. Put the panko in a shallow dish and add the chicken breasts to coat evenly with the breadcrumbs. Press the chicken gently between dry hands. If you cannot find ready-made panko, you can make your own in a food processor using a day-old (very dry) baguette.

Heat a large frying pan over a medium heat and add the oil. Fry the chicken breasts, working in small batches, for 3–4 minutes each side or until they are crisp and golden and cooked through. Add more oil if needed. Remove the breasts and set aside on kitchen paper to drain. Keep warm in a very low oven.

To make sushi vinegar cucumber ribbons, use a vegetable peeler to slice the cucumbers lengthways into long ribbons. Put the cucumber and the ginger in a serving bowl and mix with the sushi vinegar.

Squeeze out and discard any excess liquid from the cucumber mixture and serve with the chicken breasts and a wedge of lemon on the side of each plate.

YO! Sushi tip
If you are unable to find baby cucumbers, use a whole large cucumber but discard the seedy part in the middle as it is watery.

chicken katsu curry

This variation on chicken katsu is one of the best-loved items on the YO! Sushi menu. Succulent chicken encased in crispy breadcrumbs combines deliciously with a mild, Japanese-style curry sauce.

serves 4

400g (14oz) chicken thighs, boned and skinless
50g (2oz) plain flour
3 eggs
75g (3oz) panko (Japanese breadcrumbs)
50g (2oz) butter
1 onion, roughly chopped
4 tbsp mild curry powder
125ml (4½fl oz) water or chicken stock
2 tbsp soy sauce
2–3 tbsp mirin
50ml (2fl oz) vegetable oil
1½ tbsp cornflour, mixed with 3 tbsp cold water
salt and pepper
400g warm cooked rice, to serve (see pages 18–19)
4 tbsp fukujin-zuke, to serve

Preheat the oven to 120°C/250°F/gas mark ½. Dust each chicken thigh with the flour. Beat the eggs in a shallow dish and put the panko in a separate dish.

Melt the butter in a frying pan and sweat the onion over a low heat. When the onion is cooked, add the curry powder and water or chicken stock and bring to the boil. Add the soy sauce and mirin, and reduce the heat to low, leaving it to simmer for 10 minutes.

Meanwhile, dip the chicken in the egg and place on the bed of panko to coat, then pat the chicken fillets to seal the panko. Heat a frying pan over a medium heat and fry the chicken, in batches if necessary, for 5–7 minutes on each side or until crisp and golden. Lay the chicken on kitchen paper and keep warm in the oven.

Stir the cornflour paste into the sauce to thicken it and bring to a gentle boil for 2 minutes before turning off the heat. The sauce should have a yogurt-like consistency. Adjust the seasoning with salt and pepper to taste.

Cut the chicken into bite-size pieces. Divide the rice among 4 individual plates and ladle over the curry sauce, covering about half of each mound of rice. Arrange the chicken on top and serve with the fukujin-zuke on the side.

YO! Sushi tip
Fukujin-zuke is a type of Japanese pickle sold in vacuum packs in Japanese grocery stores. It is a classic accompaniment for curry dishes.

spicy chicken salad

Succulent chicken, crisp on the outside and succulent within, combined with a spicy sauce – what could be better? Covering the frying pan while the chicken is cooking is the key to keeping it moist.

serves 4

400g (14oz) chicken thighs, boned, with the skin on
1 tbsp shichimi togarashi (Japanese seven-spice chilli powder)
1 tsp salt
1 tbsp vegetable oil
4 tbsp sake
2 tbsp sweet chilli sauce
2 tsp soy sauce
4 tbsp ponzu dressing (see page 47)
200g (7oz) salad leaves of your choice
4 tbsp cress, to garnish

If you do not have a perforated lid for the frying pan you will be using, start by making a lid with a piece of foil. Cut a square piece of foil large enough to cover the pan. Fold it in half twice – you should be left with a square a quarter the size of the original. Fold the square into a triangle and repeat the process once or twice more so that you end up with a narrow triangle. Hold the triangle over the frying pan, placing the sharp point more or less above the centre of the pan. Cut the outer edge of the piece into a curve just short of the edge of the pan. Snip the pointed tip. Open out the foil: you should now have a round piece of foil with a hole in the middle.

Prick the skin of the chicken with a fork, then rub in the shichimi togarashi and salt. Heat the oil in a frying pan over a medium heat and pat the chicken dry with kitchen paper just before putting it in skin-side down. When the skin is crisp and golden, turn the chicken over to cook the other side. At the same time, add the sake, reduce the heat and cover the pan with the lid. Cook the chicken for a further 5 minutes or until the sake has evaporated and the chicken is cooked through.

Meanwhile, mix the sweet chilli sauce, soy sauce and ponzu dressing in a bowl.

Divide the salad leaves between 4 serving plates. Take the chicken out of the pan and leave it to rest on a chopping board for 5 minutes before slicing it into bite-size pieces. Arrange the chicken on top of the salad leaves. Drizzle the spicy sauce over the chicken, garnish with the cress and serve.

YO! Sushi tip
Try this recipe with duck breasts.

chicken and egg donburi

The Japanese name for this dish, *oyako-donburi*, means 'mother and child'. It takes little time to prepare and makes a satisfying one-bowl meal.

serves 4

4 large eggs
200g (7oz) boneless, skinless chicken fillets, roughly chopped
400g (14oz) warm cooked rice (see pages 18–19)
4 spring onions, finely chopped, to garnish
4 tbsp cress, to garnish

for the cooking broth
120ml (4¼fl oz) dashi stock (see page 16)
120ml (4¼fl oz) sake
4 tbsp soy sauce
4 tbsp mirin

For this recipe, the eggs have to be top quality and absolutely fresh, because they are cooked only briefly. Mix the eggs well without beating them, using a fork. Put the ingredients for the broth in a shallow saucepan over a medium heat and bring to the boil. Add the chicken and cook for 3–4 minutes or until the chicken is cooked through. Pour in the eggs and let them cook for 1 minute before you stir them. Cover and cook for another minute. The mixture should have thickened and eggs just begun to have set. Remove from the heat. Divide the rice among 4 bowls and pour the egg mixture on top. Garnish with the spring onions and cress. Serve immediately.

YO! Sushi tip
It is crucial that the eggs stay runny – so use a timer and do not over-cook them.

sesame chicken with soba noodles

This is a Japanese interpretation of the Chinese 'Bang Bang Chicken'. Not only is it delicious but you have the bonus of excellent chicken stock to use in other dishes.

serves 4

4 chicken legs
1 litre (1¾) pint water
50g (2oz) fresh root ginger, peeled and
    roughly chopped
1 onion, halved
1 carrot, scrubbed and halved
400g (14oz) dried soba noodles
2 baby cucumbers, finely shredded
2 spring onions, finely chopped, to garnish
1 tbsp toasted sesame seeds, to garnish

for the sesame dressing
100g (3½oz) toasted sesame seeds
2 tbsp sugar
1 tbsp wasabi powder
1 tbsp milk chocolate-coloured miso paste
2 tbsp mirin
2 tbsp soy sauce
4 tbsp water

Put the chicken legs, water, ginger, onion and carrot in a saucepan and bring to the boil over a medium heat. Reduce the heat once it has boiled and simmer for 30 minutes. Remove from the heat, leaving the chicken to cool in the stock.

Meanwhile, make the dressing. Grind the sesame seeds with a pestle and mortar to a smooth paste. Add the remaining dressing ingredients and grind to the consistency of yogurt, adding more water if necessary.

Take the chicken legs out of the stock. Discard the skin and bones and shred the meat with a fork. Strain the stock, discard the vegetables and keep the stock for another time.

Cook the dried soba noodles as described on page 22.

Put the chicken, soba noodles and shredded cucumber in a large bowl, add the sesame dressing (reserving 4 tablespoonfuls) and mix gently.

Arrange on 4 individual serving plates. Drizzle over the reserved sesame dressing, garnish with the chopped spring onions and toasted sesame seeds, and serve.

YO! Sushi tip
Allowing cooked chicken to cool in stock is an excellent way of keeping it moist.

soy and ginger chicken with broccoli and pumpkin

This is another delicious variation on teriyaki sauce – the ginger and rice vinegar give a light yet punchy flavour to the chicken.

serves 4

200g (7oz) pumpkin or squash, deseeded
400g (14oz) chicken thighs, boned, with skin on
4 tbsp cornflour
1 tbsp vegetable oil
4 tbsp rice vinegar
½ tbsp sugar
100g (3½oz) broccoli florets

for the cooking liquor
4 tbsp sake
4 tbsp mirin
3 tbsp sugar
4 tbsp soy sauce
2 tsp grated fresh root ginger

Cut the pumpkin into 2cm (½in) by 5cm (2in) pieces. Put in a saucepan with the sugar and enough water to cover and bring to the boil over a medium heat. Turn the heat down low when it begins to boil, cover the pan with a lid and cook for 8–10 minutes or until the pumpkin is soft. Drain, put to one side and keep warm

Lay the chicken on a chopping board skin-side down and make 3 or 4 shallow incisions. Dust the chicken with the cornflour. Heat the oil in a frying pan over a low to medium heat and place the chicken skin-side down, cooking it for 3–5 minutes or until it is crisp and golden. Turn the chicken over and cook the other side for 3 minutes. Cover the pan and turn the heat right down, leaving the chicken to steam for 3 minutes.

Remove the lid and add all the ingredients for the cooking liquor in the order given while shaking the pan to coat the chicken. When all the ingredients have been incorporated, add the rice vinegar. Remove from the heat and cover again so that it keeps warm.

Steam the broccoli for 2–3 minutes.

Cut the chicken into large, bite-size pieces and serve with the pumpkin and steamed broccoli on the side.

seared beef tataki with wasabi mashed potato

This Japanese cooking method (*tataki* literally means 'to slap') is traditionally used to cook bonito fish, but also works extremely well with meat.

450g (1lb) beef fillet – a long thin piece works
   better than a thick piece
salt and ground black pepper
100ml (3½fl oz) rice vinegar
2 punnets cress, to garnish
spring onion, to garnish (optional)

for the sauce
100ml (3½fl oz) soy sauce
20g (¾oz) fresh root ginger, peeled and grated
2 tbsp lemon juice
1 garlic clove, crushed
1 tsp sesame oil
1 tbsp toasted sesame seeds
2 spring onions, finely chopped

for the wasabi mashed potato
600g (1¼lb) all-purpose potatoes, such as Desirée
   or King Edward, peeled
50g (2oz) butter
4 tbsp mirin
1 tbsp wasabi powder, mixed to a paste with water
4 spring onions, finely chopped

For the wasabi mashed potato, chop the potatoes into small chunks and cook with just enough water to cover for 10 minutes or until soft. Drain and add the butter while the potatoes are still hot. Mash them while pouring in the mirin and wasabi paste. Continue to mash until smooth then stir in the spring onions, seasoning with salt, if needed. Cover the pan to keep the potatoes warm while you cook the meat.

Heat a heavy, cast-iron griddle pan over a high heat. Sprinkle the beef all over with a generous amount of salt and pepper and rub it in. Sear the beef in the griddle for 1 minute each side, until both sides are browned. Transfer the beef to a chopping board, cut into thin slices, then place in a non-metallic dish and pour over the rice vinegar. Put each slice on a chopping board and slap with the palm of your hand – this tenderises the meat.

Make the sauce by mixing all the ingredients in a bowl.

Arrange the meat on 4 plates, drizzle over the sauce, garnish with cress and spring onion, and serve with the wasabi mashed potatoes on the side.

YO! Sushi tip
Try this method of cooking with lamb fillet or tuna.

teriyaki beef steak donburi

Donburi is the Japanese equivalent of cheese on toast – quick, easy and satisfying! It is the perfect one-bowl meal and almost anything, from fish to chicken or beef, can be served on top of the steaming hot rice.

serves 4

2 garlic cloves, crushed
100ml (3½fl oz) teriyaki sauce (see page 40)
½ tbsp vegetable oil
4 beef sirloin or fillet steaks, each weighing about 100g (3½oz)
400g (14oz) warm cooked rice (see pages 18–19)
2 bunches pak choi, roughly chopped and lightly steamed
4 spring onions, finely chopped
2 tsp wasabi paste

In a shallow, flat-based dish, mix the garlic and teriyaki sauce and set aside.

Heat the oil in a frying pan over a high heat until it is very hot and almost smoking, then add the steaks. Turn them over when the top, uncooked side is beginning to turn pale, at which point, turn them over, and cover and cook for 1 minute (for medium rare) or 2 minutes (for medium). Remove the steaks from the pan and immerse them in the teriyaki sauce for 5 minutes, turning them over from time to time. Cut the beef into slices 2.5cm (1in) thick and set aside the teriyaki sauce for later.

Divide the cooked rice among 4 bowls and arrange the steaks and pak choi on top. Drizzle over the reserved teriyaki sauce, sprinkle with the chopped spring onions and place a small dollop of wasabi paste on top of each bowl. Serve immediately.

YO! Sushi tip
This recipe works equally well with lamb or chicken fillets.

beef curry

Curries are very popular in Japan and were first introduced in the middle of the nineteenth century, via England. A number of Japanese food manufacturers sell different kinds of instant curry sauce. Resembling chocolate bars, they contain all the necessary spices, seasonings and stocks – but this recipe is designed to make a Japanese-type curry without using instant sauce. Japanese curries are generally mild – quite sweet and creamy. Adjust the amount of honey and curry powder to suit your taste.

serves 4

2 tbsp vegetable oil
25g (1oz) butter
2 onions, peeled and roughly chopped
400g (14oz) braising or stewing beef, diced
75g (3oz) plain flour
1 carrot, peeled and roughly cut into chunks
2 medium potatoes, peeled and roughly cut into chunks
700ml (1¼ pints) beef stock
3–4 tbsp medium curry powder
1 apple, peeled and grated
1–2 tbsp clear honey
1–2 tbsp Worcestershire sauce
salt and ground black pepper
400g (14oz) warm cooked rice (see pages 18–19)

Heat the oil and butter in a large saucepan over a medium heat and fry the onion until soft but not browned. Dust the beef with the flour. When the onions are soft, add the beef and brown it, stirring constantly to prevent the onions from burning. Add the carrot and potatoes, and continue to cook for a further 3–5 minutes before adding the beef stock. Bring the stock to the boil, reduce the heat to low and add the curry powder, apple, honey and Worcestershire sauce. Cover and simmer for 45 minutes. Season with salt and pepper.

Divide the cooked rice among 4 serving plates, ladle the curry over it and serve.

chicken ramen

Ramen are Chinese-style egg noodles that are available dried or in soft form in vacuum packs. This recipe uses dried ramen noodles, which should be cooked in the same way as other Japanese noodles (see page 22), then lightly tossed in a few drops of sesame oil to stop them sticking together.

serves 4

for the soup
1.5 litres (2¾ pints) chicken stock
2 garlic cloves, peeled and grated
50g (2oz) fresh root ginger, peeled and grated
250g (9oz) milk chocolate-coloured miso paste
salt and soy sauce (optional)

for the chicken noodles
2 tbsp vegetable oil
1 onion, thinly sliced
200g (7oz) skinless chicken breast, thinly sliced on the diagonal
1 leek, thinly sliced
1 carrot, peeled and shredded
4 tbsp frozen sweetcorn
1 small can bamboo shoots in matchstick form, drained
200g (7oz) beansprouts
4 tbsp soy sauce
1 tsp ground white pepper
400g (14oz) dried ramen noodles, cooked, coated lightly in sesame oil and kept warm
2 tsp chilli oil
2 tsp toasted sesame seeds

To make the soup, heat the chicken stock with the garlic and ginger over a medium heat. Bring the soup almost to boiling point and add the miso gradually until it has all dissolved. Turn the heat up but take off the stove as soon as it has boiled. Season with salt and soy sauce if necessary, and cover the saucepan to keep it warm.

To make the chicken noodles, heat a wok over a medium to high heat for 2–3 minutes, then pour in the oil and wait 1–2 minutes before adding the onion. Stir-fry the onion until soft, then add the chicken. Cook the chicken for 2–3 minutes, then add all the vegetables except the beansprouts and stir-fry for 2–3 minutes. Add the beansprouts, toss to combine and immediately remove from the heat. Drizzle the soy sauce along the side of the wok, sprinkle in the white pepper and toss the ingredients together.

Divide the cooked ramen noodles among 4 bowls. Reheat the soup to just below boiling point and ladle over the noodles. Top with the chicken and vegetables, chilli oil and sesame seeds, and serve immediately.

YO! Sushi tip
This recipe may seem rather long and complicated, involving a number of different cooking styles, but if you prepare all the ingredients and your equipment first, you'll find it far easier.

Try this recipe with beef: replace the chicken stock with beef stock and swap the leek for thinly sliced green pepper.

prawn yakisoba

Yakisoba is a popular stir-fry noodle dish that is simple to make. Soft, semi-cooked Chinese-style egg noodles are sold in vacuum packs in supermarkets, often labelled 'stir-fry noodles'.

serves 4

4 caps dried shiitake mushrooms, soaked in
   4 tablespoons warm water until soft
400g (14oz) raw tiger prawns, shelled
2 tbsp vegetable oil
1 onion, thinly sliced
1 carrot, peeled and thinly sliced
2 garlic cloves, peeled and sliced
2 tsp finely chopped fresh root ginger,
200g (7oz) pointed cabbage, chopped
1 tsp toasted sesame oil
500g (1lb 2oz) soft, stir-fry noodles
6 tbsp yakisoba sauce (see page 41)
4 tbsp finely chopped spring onions, to garnish
2 tbsp dried shredded nori, to garnish (optional)

Remove the shiitake mushrooms from the water and gently squeeze them (reserving the soaking liquid). Discard the stems and slice the caps. Run the tip of a small kitchen knife along the backs of the prawns to remove their black veins.

Heat a wok over a medium to high heat and add the vegetable oil. When the oil is hot, stir-fry the onion for 2–3 minutes. Add the carrot, garlic, ginger, cabbage and prawns, and cook for 3–4 minutes or until the prawns begin to turn pink. Using a slotted spoon, remove the vegetables and prawns from the wok. Add the sesame oil and the noodles, gently separating the strands with your fingers. Stir-fry the noodles for 1–2 minutes, strain the reserved shiitake soaking liquid and add to the pan. Return the vegetables and prawns to the wok and add the yakisoba sauce. Toss and stir to mix for a further 2–3 minutes.

Divide the noodles among 4 plates, garnish with the chopped spring onions and shredded nori, and serve immediately.

salmon nanban zuke

The Chinese characters used to write *nanban* mean 'southern barbarians' – this originally referred to Indo-China but later included other southeastern countries such as Thailand and Malaysia. For culinary purposes, *nanban* describes food flavoured with onions and chillies.

4 salmon fillets, each weighing 100g (3¹/₂oz)
1 tsp salt
1 red onion, peeled and thinly sliced
1 carrot, peeled and cut into matchsticks
400g (14oz) warm cooked rice (see pages 18–19)
1 punnet cress, to garnish
2 tbsp shredded nori, to garnish

for the stock
400ml (14fl oz) dashi stock (see page 16)
2 tbsp rice vinegar
2 tbsp soy sauce
2 tbsp sake
1 large red chilli, cut lengthways and deseeded

Cut each salmon fillet into 3 pieces, sprinkle with the salt and set aside.

Put all the stock ingredients in a saucepan and bring to the boil slowly so the chilli has time to infuse. Add the onion and carrot and simmer for 1 minute. Place the pieces of salmon in a sieve and immerse them in the stock. Poach for 2–3 minutes, then turn off the heat and remove the chilli.

Spoon the cooked rice into 4 serving bowls and place 3 slices of salmon on top of each. Ladle the stock over the top, garnish with the cress and shredded nori and serve.

YO! Sushi tip
Try using other fish such as sea bass, bream or sole.

beef udon

Udon are the thick, white noodles made from wheat flour that are popular in the southwest of Japan. You can buy udon noodles either in dried form or semi-cooked in vacuum packs from supermarkets. Silky yet gutsy, udon noodles make a perfect partner for beef.

serves 4

1 tbsp vegetable oil
200g (7oz) silverside beef, very thinly sliced
2 tbsp plain flour
2 leeks, trimmed and very thinly sliced
400g (14oz) cooked udon noodles (see page 22), kept warm
spring onion, to garnish (optional)
shichimi togarashi (Japanese seven-spice chilli powder), to serve

for the broth
3 litres (5¼ pints) dashi stock (see page 16)
4 tbsp sugar
50ml (2fl oz) mirin
100ml (3½fl oz) soy sauce

Heat the oil in a heavy-based saucepan over a medium to high heat. Dust the slices of beef with the flour. Add the beef. Cook for 2–3 minutes, shaking the pan constantly.

Mix together all the ingredients for the broth and pour into the saucepan to join the beef. Bring to the boil, scooping off any scum that floats to the surface. Reduce the heat to low, add the leeks and cook for 3–5 minutes.

Divide the cooked udon noodles among 4 bowls, ladle in the beef soup, garnish with the spring onion and serve immediately. Offer around the shichimi togarashi.

YO! Sushi tip
If you are using semi-cooked udon, they need to be refreshed in a bowl of boiling water for 2–3 minutes, stirring constantly with a pair of chopsticks or a fork to separate the strands.

Try adding some reconstituted dried shiitake mushrooms to the broth for extra flavour.

sashimi

Sashimi is the freshest and best-quality fish or shellfish served raw. Unlike sushi, sashimi is not served with rice but sliced into thicker pieces and served with wasabi and soy sauce. Good sashimi depends not only on the cook's preparation and presentation skills but also on their ability to select the best, freshest fish. Because there is no cooking involved, the quality of the fish is paramount (read about how to choose fish on page 23). See pages 24–25 for step-by-step instructions on slicing sashimi. Here are some pointers for producing wonderful sashimi at home.

how to serve a plate of sashimi

A plate of sashimi is typically served with a garnish, such as daikon salad (see page 181), shiso leaves, slices of lime or lemon and a few sprigs of cress. A small amount of wasabi and a small dish of soy sauce for dipping are served on the side.

If you are serving just one variety of fish, allow 3 or 5 pieces per person (Japanese people do not like 4 as the word for 4 in Japanese sounds like the word for death and is considered inauspicious), and allow 2 or 3 pieces if there are more than 2 types of fish.

Place a small mound of shredded daikon off-centre on a plate and arrange the fish on the side. Use a slice of lime or lemon as a divider between the different varieties of fish. To eat, dab a tiny amount of wasabi on a slice of fish and dip a corner into the soy sauce.

wafer-thin lemon sole

White flat fish is particularly suited to very thinly cut sashimi – the cut brings out the delicate texture of flat fish.

serves 4

400g (14oz) lemon sole fillets, skin removed
½ lemon, cut into 8 half-moon slices
wasabi and soy sauce, to serve

With a very sharp knife held at a 30 degree angle, slice the fish as thinly as possible (see pictures on page 24). Divide the slices into 4 equal portions and arrange them on 4 plates. Put 2 lemon slices on each plate and serve with a small mound of wasabi on the side and soy sauce in separate dishes.

sesame-seared salmon

This is a variation on salmon sashimi. A thin crunchy crust of sesame seeds adds extra taste and texture.

serves 4

40g (1 1/2 oz) mixed black and white toasted
  sesame seeds
1 tsp ground black pepper
1/2 tsp sea salt
400g (14oz) salmon fillet, skin removed
200g (7oz) daikon salad (see page 181)
1 tsp sesame oil
1 tsp vegetable oil
1 tbsp cress, to garnish
wasabi and soy sauce, to serve

Crush the sesame seeds with a pestle and mortar, and mix with the pepper and salt. Spread the mixture on a shallow tray or dish and coat the salmon fillets on both sides, using your hands to press the sesame mixture onto the fish. Set aside. Arrange the daikon on 4 individual serving plates.

Heat a non-stick frying pan over a medium heat and add the 2 oils. When the oils are very hot, sear the salmon for no longer than 30 seconds on each side, just to seal it. Take the fish off the heat and set aside to rest before cutting into sashimi slices (see instructions on page 24).

Arrange the salmon slices on top of the shredded daikon, allowing 3 or 5 slices per person. Garnish each plate with 1/2 teaspoon of cress and serve with a small mound of wasabi on the side and soy sauce in separate dipping dishes.

YO! Sushi tip
This recipe works equally well with tuna.

beetroot salmon

The beetroot marinade gives the salmon a stunning red colour as well as a touch of sweetness.

serves 4

for the marinade
200ml (7fl oz) sushi vinegar (see page 20)
2 tbsp light soy sauce
1 tbsp caster sugar (optional)

2 raw beetroot, peeled and shredded
400g (14oz) salmon fillet
200g (7oz) daikon salad (see page 181)
1/2 lemon, cut into 8 half-moon slices
wasabi and soy sauce, to serve

Mix all the ingredients for the marinade in a shallow glass or non-metallic dish. If you like a sweeter taste, use the sugar. Add the shredded beetroot and salmon to the marinade. Leave to marinate for 2–3 hours.

Arrange the daikon in mounds on 4 individual serving plates. Take the salmon out of the marinade and pat it dry with kitchen paper. Cut the salmon into sashimi slices (see instructions on page 24) and arrange 3 or 5 slices per person next to the daikon mounds with 2 slices of lemon as dividers. Serve with a small mound of wasabi on the side and individual dishes of soy sauce.

coriander-seared tuna

YO! Sushi use the freshest 'sashimi-grade' yellowfin tuna lion for their tuna sashimi, although tuna steak is perfect for home use.

serves 4

400g (14oz) tuna steak
1 tbsp vegetable oil
200g (7oz) daikon salad (see page 181)
1 lime, cut into 8 slices
2 tbsp cress, to garnish
wasabi and soy sauce, to serve

for the crust
2 tbsp ground coriander
50g (2oz) fresh coriander, finely chopped
1 tsp fine sea salt
1 tsp ground black pepper

Cut the tuna into 3 blocks of equal thickness. To make the crust, put the ground coriander in a pan and dry roast for 30 seconds over a medium heat. Brush the tuna with a little of the oil. Mix together all the ingredients and use your hands to press the mixture all over the tuna.

Heat a non-stick frying pan and add the remaining oil. When the pan is very hot, sear the tuna, cooking for no longer than 30 seconds on each side, just enough to seal the outside. Remove the tuna from the pan and set aside to cool and rest.

When the tuna has cooled to room temperature, slice each block into 1cm (½in) thick sashimi pieces (see instructions on page 25).

Arrange the daikon in neat mounds on 4 individual serving plates. Place 3 or 5 slices of tuna next to each daikon mound with 2 slices of lime as dividers. Garnish with the cress and serve with a small mound of wasabi on the side and soy sauce in separate dipping bowls.

tuna tataki

This is a simple but tasty dish of seared tuna with sesame seeds. Easy to prepare, it is full of flavour and has a pleasingly crunchy texture.

serves 4

400g (14oz) tuna steak
3 tbsp vegetable oil
100g (3½oz) rocket leaves
wasabi paste and soy sauce

for the crust
40g (1½oz) black and white toasted sesame seeds, crushed
2 tsp freshly ground black pepper
1 tsp sea salt

Cut the tuna into 3 equal blocks and brush them with 1 tablespoon of the vegetable oil. Mix together the ingredients for the crust and cover the tuna blocks.

Heat the remaining oil in a non-stick frying pan and sear the tuna pieces for no more than 30 seconds on each side, just to seal them. Take the tuna out of the pan and set aside to cool to room temperature before slicing into sashimi pieces (see instructions on page 25).

Pile up the rocket leaves on 4 individual serving plates and arrange the tuna pieces next to the rocket. Each person should have 3 or 5 slices of tuna.

Serve with a small mound of wasabi paste on the side and individual dishes of soy sauce.

tokyo-style chirashi sushi

This style of sushi is a natural extension of sashimi – a few slices of sashimi served on top of sushi rice. You may choose any combination of fish and seafood and arrange them however you like, but do try to alternate colours and shapes – this dish should be a feast for the eyes as well as the mouth. See pages 23–25 for advice on buying fish as well as cutting sashimi.

serves 4

400g (14oz) prepared sushi rice (see page 19–21)
4 tbsp daikon salad (see page 181)
4 tsp cress
150g (5oz) tuna steak, cut into 8 sashimi pieces
150g (5oz) white fish fillets of your choice, cut into 8 sashimi pieces (see page 24)
150g (5oz) salmon fillets, cut into 8 sashimi pieces
4 prepared tiger prawns (see page 184)
4 scallops, coral removed, sliced in half
4 tsp salmon roe
1 baby cucumber, cut into 12 diagonal slices
½ Japanese rolled omelette, cut into 8 pieces (see page 110)
4 tsp wasabi paste
soy sauce, to serve

Divide the prepared sushi rice among 4 individual bowls and fill each two-thirds full with the sushi rice – the idea is to cover the surface of the rice with a colourful arrangement of sashimi pieces.

Heap a tablespoon of the daikon salad on the far side of each bowl and put a teaspoon of cress next to it. Carefully arrange the slices of fish and shellfish, roe, cucumber and omelette as you wish (see picture opposite for inspiration). Put a small mound of wasabi paste in the corner. Serve with a small dish of soy sauce for dipping.

hand rolls

Hand rolls or *temaki* are cornet-shaped rolls traditionally eaten at the sushi counter as fast as the chef can make them. They are also perfect for sushi parties. Having prepared some sushi rice, cut different kinds of fillings into a pencil shape and lay them out on a large plate. Then show your guests how it is done and let them make their own. They'll love it! See pages 26–27 for step-by-step rolling instructions. Each of the following recipes makes 1 hand roll.

salmon and avocado

1 heaped tbsp prepared sushi rice (see pages 19–21)
$1/2$ nori sheet
1 thin slice of avocado
2 strips salmon, approximately 9cm (3in) long
1 tsp ginger wasabi mayonnaise (see page 42)
$1/4$ tsp white toasted sesame seeds
$1/4$ tsp black sesame seeds

Place the sushi rice on the nori. Put the avocado and salmon strips on the rice and spread over the wasabi mayonnaise. Sprinkle with the sesame seeds and make a cornet as described on pages 26–27.

spicy tuna

1 heaped tbsp prepared sushi rice (see pages 19–21)
$1/2$ nori sheet
2 tbsp tuna trimmings
$1/2$ spring onion, finely chopped
$1/2$ tsp shichimi togarashi (Japanese seven-spice chilli powder)

Place the sushi rice on the nori. Mix together the tuna, spring onion and shichimi togarashi for the filling. Make a cornet as described on pages 26–27.

crispy salmon skin

1 heaped tbsp prepared sushi rice (see pages
   19–21)
$\frac{1}{2}$ nori sheet
$\frac{1}{4}$ tsp salt
$\frac{1}{2}$ postcard-size piece of salmon skin
$\frac{1}{4}$ tsp wasabi paste
$\frac{1}{2}$ spring onion, finely chopped
3 rocket leaves

Place the sushi rice on the nori. Sprinkle the salt
over the salmon skin and grill until it becomes
crisp. Cut the skin into thin strips and mix in a
bowl with the wasabi paste, spring onion and
rocket leaves. Make a cornet as described on
pages 26–27.

vegetarian

1 heaped tbsp prepared sushi rice (see pages
   19–21)
$\frac{1}{2}$ nori sheet
3 pencil-shape pieces cucumber, 9cm (3$\frac{1}{2}$in) long
3 pencil-shape pieces carrot, 9cm (3$\frac{1}{2}$in) long
1 asparagus spear, lightly steamed
$\frac{1}{2}$ tsp white toasted sesame seeds

Place the sushi rice on the nori. Place the
cucumber, carrot and asparagus pieces in
the centre of the rice and sprinkle over a few
sesame seeds. Make a cornet as described
on pages 26–27.

crab and avocado

1 heaped tbsp prepared sushi rice (see pages
   19–21)
$\frac{1}{2}$ nori sheet
1 tsp ginger wasabi mayonnaise (see page 42)
3 tsp cooked white crabmeat
1 pencil-shape slice avocado
1 tsp spring onion, finely chopped
$\frac{1}{2}$ tsp toasted sesame seeds

Place the sushi rice on the nori. Spread the
mayonnaise down the centre of the rice and
place the crabmeat and avocado on top.
Sprinkle over the spring onion and sesame
seeds. Make a cornet as shown on pages
26–27.

tempura prawn and wild rocket

1 heaped tbsp prepared sushi rice (see pages
   19–21)
$\frac{1}{2}$ nori sheet
1 tempura prawn (see page 168)
3 tsp pickled sushi ginger, finely sliced
5 wild rocket leaves

Place the sushi rice on the nori. Place the prawn
in the middle of the rice with the ginger and
rocket leaves. Make a cornet as described on
pages 26–27.

smoked salmon and salmon roe pressed sushi

Pressed sushi was very popular all over Japan until the early nineteenth century when nigiri sushi was invented in Tokyo. Traditional pressed sushi requires wooden moulds of varying sizes and shapes that are difficult to find outside Japan. Use a cooking ring or a pastry cutter instead. Makes 1 pressed sushi.

2 slices smoked salmon
80g (3¼oz) prepared sushi rice (see pages 19–21)
½ tsp wasabi paste
3 tsp salmon roe
1 tsp sake
½ tsp soy sauce
1 tsp cress
2 tbsp ginger wasabi mayonnaise (see page 42)

Cut the smoked salmon into 2 circles using a cooking ring or pastry cutter. Divide the sushi rice into 2 equal portions. Wet the cooking ring with water and place it in the centre of a plate. With a moistened serving spoon, put half the rice in the ring and pat it down to fill the mould. Spread over the wasabi paste and place a smoked salmon circle on top. Spoon in the rest of the rice to make a second layer and pat it down. Gently lift the ring while pressing the rice with the back of a spoon.

Put another smoked salmon circle on top. If you wish, make a rose out of the salmon trimmings and place on the mound. Mix the salmon roe with the sake and soy sauce and spoon over the rose – don't worry if some falls down. Sprinkle the cress over the roe, drizzle with the wasabi mayonnaise and serve.

YO! Sushi tip

This makes a most elegant starter. Keep the wasabi mayonnaise in a squeezable plastic bottle with a nozzle so you can create attractive patterns.

maki

Maki zushi or 'rolled sushi' is Japan's answer to sandwiches. Like sandwiches, the origins of maki are said to lie in gambling dens, where keen gamblers who couldn't bear to leave the table in search of food took to wrapping their snacks in nori and rice. Maki is highly versatile and portable, and when made properly it is beautiful. As with many good things in life, however, practice makes perfect. So be patient if your early attempts are not as good as those you enjoy at YO! Sushi.

Maki comes in a variety of different thickness, ranging from hoso maki (a thin roll with a single filling) to futomaki (a thick roll with several different fillings, see page 153). The basic technique is the same, though. You can choose any filling you like, but here are some classic suggestions to start you off. See pages 28–29 for step-by-step rolling instructions. Each recipe makes 1 roll (6 pieces when cut).

asparagus

1–2 asparagus spears
65g (2^{1}/$_{4}$oz) prepared sushi rice (see pages 19–21)
^{1}/$_{2}$ nori sheet
^{1}/$_{2}$ tsp toasted sesame seeds

Steam the asparagus for 1–2 minutes and refresh in a bowl of cold water. Spread the sushi rice over the nori, remembering to leave a margin of 1cm (^{1}/$_{2}$in) at the top edge of the nori uncovered (see page 28). Place the asparagus in the centre of the rice, sprinkle over the sesame seeds and roll. Do not worry if the tips of the asparagus stick out – they look pretty. Cut the roll into 6 equal pieces and serve.

avocado

65g (2^{1}/$_{4}$oz) prepared sushi rice (see pages 19–21)
^{1}/$_{2}$ nori sheet
^{1}/$_{4}$ avocado, peeled and cut into thin strips
^{1}/$_{2}$ tbsp ginger wasabi mayonnaise (see page 42)

Spread the sushi rice over the nori, remembering to leave a margin of 1cm (^{1}/$_{2}$in) at the top edge of the nori uncovered (see page 28). Place the avocado in the centre of the rice then spread the wasabi over the top. Roll and cut into 6 equal pieces and serve.

sushi omelette

¼ Japanese rolled omelette (see page 110)
65g (2¼oz) prepared sushi rice (see pages 19–21)
½ nori sheet

Cut the omelette into pencil-size strips for the filling. Spread the sushi rice over the nori, remembering to leave a margin of 1cm (½in) at the top edge of the nori uncovered (see page 28). Place the omelette in the centre of the rice. Roll and cut into 6 equal pieces and serve.

cucumber

65g (2¼oz) prepared sushi rice (see pages 19–21)
½ nori sheet
a dab of wasabi paste
a strip of cucumber, the thickness of a pencil, cut to fit the width of the nori sheet
½ tsp toasted sesame seeds

Spread the sushi rice evenly over the nori, leaving a margin of 1cm (½in) at the top edge of the nori uncovered (see page 28). Smear a dab of wasabi along the middle of the rice and place the cucumber strip on top of that. Sprinkle the sesame seeds along the cucumber. Roll the maki and shape it into a square cylinder. Cut into 6 equal pieces and serve.

tuna

½ nori sheet
65g (2¼oz) prepared sushi rice (see pages 19–21)
a dab of wasabi paste
20g (¾oz) tuna steak, cut into 1 long or 2 short, strips

Spread the sushi rice over the nori, leaving a margin of 1cm (½in) at the top edge of the nori uncovered (see page 28). Spread the wasabi along the centre of the rice and place the tuna over the top. Roll and cut into 6 equal pieces.

smoked salmon and chive

½ nori sheet
1 slice smoked salmon
5–7 chives
65g (2¼oz) prepared sushi rice (see pages 19–21)
a dab of wasabi paste

Spread the smoked salmon on a chopping board and trim to make it 2cm (¾in) long and the same width as the nori, using the trimmings to make up the width. Lay the chives across the width of the salmon and roll to make a tube. Make a maki as for cucumber maki using the smoked salmon and chive roll as a single filling.

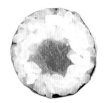

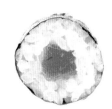

inside-out rolls (ISO)

Uramaki, literally 'inside-out roll', or 'ISO', is a relative newcomer and is said to have been invented in America for the benefit of a sushi fan who disliked the feel of crisp nori in his mouth. True or not, this is one of YO! Sushi's most popular types of sushi. It is easier to make than you would think and more suited to being made in advance than traditional maki that have the nori on the outside. See pages 30–31 for step-by-step rolling instructions. Each recipe makes 1 roll (8 pieces when cut).

YO! roll

½ nori sheet
175g (6oz) prepared sushi rice (see pages 19–21)
100g (3½oz) salmon fillet, cut into finger-thick strips
50g (2oz) avocado, cut into strips (less than 1 avocado)
1 tbsp ginger wasabi mayonnaise (see page 42)
1 heaped tbsp tobiko (flying-fish roe)

Place the nori sheet on a rolling mat covered with cling film. Cover the whole sheet of nori with sushi rice and turn it over. Place the strips of salmon across the middle of the nori, lay the avocado either side and drizzle with the wasabi mayonnaise. Roll the ISO as described on pages 30–31. Spread the tobiko on a large plate and roll the ISO in it to coat evenly. Cut into 8 equal pieces and serve.

california

½ nori sheet
175g (6oz) prepared sushi rice (see pages 19–21)
a dab of wasabi paste
60g (2¼oz) avocado, cut into strips (less than 1 avocado)
4–5 crabsticks
½ tbsp toasted black sesame seeds
½ tbsp toasted white sesame seeds

Place the nori sheet on a rolling mat covered with cling film. Cover the whole sheet of nori with sushi rice and turn it over so that the nori side is uppermost. Spread the wasabi over the middle of the nori, place the strips of avocado on top of the wasabi and lay the crabsticks along each side. Roll the ISO as described on pages 30–31). Spread the black and white sesame seeds on a large plate and roll the ISO in them to coat. Cut the ISO into 8 slices and serve.

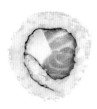    

crispy salmon skin and spring onion

½ nori sheet
175g (6oz) prepared sushi rice (see pages 19–21)
a dab of wasabi paste
200g (7oz) crispy salmon skin (see page 146),
    cut into thin strips
2 spring onions, finely chopped
10g (½oz) mizuna or rocket

Place the nori on a rolling mat covered with cling film. Cover the whole sheet of nori with sushi rice and turn it over so that the nori side is uppermost. Smear the wasabi over the middle of the nori, and lay the strips of salmon skin on top of the wasabi. Spread the spring onions along one side of the salmon skin and the mizuna or rocket leaves along the other. Roll the ISO as described on pages 30–31, cut into 8 equal slices and serve.

spicy chicken

½ nori sheet
175g (6oz) prepared sushi rice (see pages 19–21)
1 chicken katsu (see page 120), sliced into strips
20g (¾oz) mizuna or rocket leaves
½ tbsp garlic chilli sauce
1 tbsp mayonnaise
1 tbsp shichimi togarashi (Japanese seven-spice
    chilli powder)
1 tbsp BBQ sauce (optional)

Place the nori on a rolling mat covered with cling film. Cover the whole sheet of nori with sushi rice and turn it over so that the nori side is uppermost. Put the chicken katsu across the middle of the nori and the mizuna or rocket leaves on one side. Drizzle the garlic chilli sauce over the strips of chicken katsu and make a line of mayonnaise beside the chicken, the opposite side from the mizuna. Sprinkle the shichimi togarashi over the fillings and roll to make an ISO (see pages 30–31). Cut the ISO into 8 equal slices and, if you like, drizzle some BBQ sauce over the slices before serving.

vegetable

½ nori sheet
175g (6oz) prepared sushi rice (see pages 19–21)
½ rolled omelette (see page 110), cut into strips
½ tbsp good-quality mayonnaise
60g (2¼oz) avocado, cut into pencil-size strips
1 medium-thick vine tomato, halved, deseeded and
    cut into pencil-thick strips
½ baby cucumber, cut into pencil-thick strips

Place the nori on a rolling mat covered with cling film. Cover the whole sheet of nori with sushi rice and turn it over so that the nori side is uppermost. Place the omelette across the middle of the nori and drizzle a line of mayonnaise on top of it. Arrange the avocado along one side of the omelette, then put the tomato topped with the cucumber along the other side. Roll the ISO as decribed on pages 30–31 and cut into 8 slices.

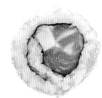

dragon roll

Even in Japan, home cooks buy ready-prepared eel, which comes coated in a sweet soy-based sauce – cooking eels is a special skill that is best left to the experts. Outside Japan, grilled eels are sold in vacuum packs in Japanese grocery stores. Defrost thoroughly before using.

makes 1 roll (8 pieces when cut)

½ nori sheet
175g (6oz) prepared sushi rice (see pages 19–21)
4 tbsp cooked white crabmeat
⅓ avocado, peeled, stoned and cut into strips
20g (¾oz) mizuna or rocket
1 piece cucumber, skin on, pencil-thick, 18cm (7in) long
1 tbsp ginger wasabi mayonnaise (see page 42)
1 grilled eel fillet, trimmed to 18cm (7in) long
1 tsp sansho (Japanese white pepper)

Place the nori on a rolling mat covered with cling film. Cover the whole sheet of nori with sushi rice and turn it over so that the nori side is uppermost. Put the crabmeat across the middle of the nori and the avocado wedges along one side. Place the mizuna or rocket and cucumber along the other side of the crabmeat and drizzle the wasabi mayonnaise over the fillings. Roll to make an ISO (see pages 30–31). Wrap the eel around the ISO and sprinkle with the sansho. Cut into 8 equal slices and serve.

vegetable futomaki

Traditional futomaki (thick roll) once used two sheets of nori with up to seven or eight varieties of fillings. It was quite substantial – two or three slices would easily have satisfied a hungry man – and was cumbersome to eat. The size of sushi portions in general became smaller as Japanese women started to eat out after the Second World War and eating larger pieces was seen to be unladylike. Today's futomaki is actually what used to be called chu maki (a medium roll), and uses half a sheet of nori with up to six kinds of fillings.

Try any combination of fillings you like and extend your repertoire as you become more accomplished.

makes 1 roll (8 pieces when cut)

4 dried shiitake mushrooms
1/2 nori sheet
130g (4 1/2oz) prepared sushi rice (see pages 19–21)
1/2 Japanese rolled omelette (see page 110), finger-thick, 18cm (7in) long
1/4 avocado, sliced
2 asparagus spears, lightly steamed
1/2 cooked beetroot, cut into matchstick-sized pieces
1 finger-thick piece cucumber, 18cm (7in) long

Soak the dried shiitake mushrooms in a small bowl of tepid water for 10 minutes, then cook in the water over a medium heat for 10 minutes. Discard the stalks. Thinly slice the caps.

Place a sheet of nori shiny-side down on a rolling mat. Spread the sushi rice over the nori leaving a 2.5cm (1in) margin at the top. Place the strip of omelette across the centre of the rice and add the remaining fillings. Roll as for ISO (see instructions on pages 30–31). Cut into 8 equal slices and serve.

YO! Sushi tip
Try a combination of cucumber, kampyo (dried strips of gourd), omelette and red pepper.

YO! Sushi's rice pudding

The addition of some sweet adzuki bean jam gives this traditional western dessert a Japanese twist.

serves 4

200g (7oz) pudding rice
50g (2oz) adzuki beans
2 litres (3½ pints) water
200g (7oz) soft light brown sugar
1 vanilla pod
100ml (3½fl oz) soya milk
½ tsp salt
4 tbsp ready-made, sweet adzuki bean jam

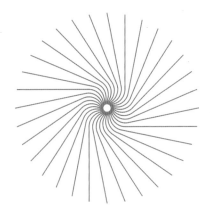

Start by washing the rice in several changes of water until the water runs clear. Put the rice and adzuki beans in a large saucepan with the water and leave to soak overnight.

Cover the saucepan and bring to the boil over a low heat, then adjust the lid slightly to allow the steam to escape and simmer for 1 hour. Add the sugar and vanilla pod, and simmer for a further 30 minutes or until the rice and adzuki beans are soft and much of the water has disappeared.

Add the soya milk and salt to the rice mixture and bring it back to the boil. Leave to simmer for another 10 minutes then remove from the heat. Remove the vanilla pod.

Divide the rice among 4 serving bowls, top each with a tablespoon of adzuki bean jam and serve immediately.

YO! Sushi tip
Sweet adzuki bean jam is called *an* in Japanese and is sold in cans in Japanese grocery stores. Alternatively, serve the rice pudding with chopped bananas or strawberries.

chocolate mousse with ginger

This deliciously rich mousse is made from chocolate and ginger and is perfect for any occasion, from informal Sunday lunches for family and friends to special dinner parties when you want to impress. Because it can be made in advance, it is perfect for entertaining.

serves 4

2 egg yolks
200ml (7fl oz) milk
2 tsp grated fresh root ginger
30g (1oz) caster sugar
½ tbsp gelatine powder
100g (3½oz) good-quality plain chocolate, roughly chopped
225ml (8fl oz) double or whipping cream
2 tbsp dry crystallised ginger, chopped, to decorate

In a large non-stick saucepan, beat the egg yolks, milk, grated ginger and sugar until blended. Sprinkle the gelatine powder evenly over the mixture, leave to stand for 5 minutes to soften the gelatine, then add the chopped chocolate.

Heat the mixture over a low heat for about 10 minutes, stirring frequently with a wooden spoon, or until the gelatine has dissolved, the chocolate has melted and the mixture has thickened. Do not let it boil or it will curdle. Take the saucepan off the heat and pour the contents into a bowl. Cover and chill for about 1 hour, stirring occasionally, or until the mixture has begun to set a little.

Whip the cream until stiff peaks form and, with a rubber spatula, fold the whipped cream into the chocolate mixture. Transfer the mousse to 4 individual soufflé dishes, cover and chill for 3 hours or until set.

Before serving, decorate with the chopped crystallised ginger.

japanese fruit with soya yogurt

This beautiful, layered, fresh fruit salad has a delightul Japanese flavour. Try serving it in glasses so that your guests can enjoy the sight as well as the taste of it.

serves 4

4 tbsp mirin
1 tbsp yuzu juice or lime juice
2 ripe persimmon, peeled and diced
4 kiwi fruits, peeled and sliced
2 ripe white peaches, peeled and diced
16 strawberries, washed and sliced
$\frac{1}{2}$ tsp matcha (green tea powder), to decorate

for the topping
125ml (4$\frac{1}{2}$fl oz) double or whipping cream
1 tbsp icing sugar, sifted
1 tsp yuzu juice or lime juice
125ml (4$\frac{1}{2}$fl oz) soya yogurt

Mix the mirin and yuzu juice in a small bowl and place 4 glasses in the freezer to chill.

Put the different fruit in separate bowls, drizzle over the mixture and turn gently to mix. Leave the fruit to macerate while you make the yogurt topping.

Whip the double cream with the icing sugar and the yuzu juice until stiff peaks form. With a rubber spatula, fold in the soya yogurt until evenly blended.

Roughly divide each kind of fruit into 4 portions and spoon into the glasses, beginning with the persimmon and following with the kiwi, peaches and strawberries, in that order. Top each glass with the yogurt mixture, sift over the matcha and serve.

YO! Sushi tip
Yuzu juice is sold in green bottles from Japanese grocery shops. It is rather expensive but a little goes a long way and it will keep for 8 weeks in the refrigerator.

If you can't find persimmon, use sharon fruit or mango.

samurai

find your inner expert

clear soup with swirling egg and spinach

This is a delicate and sophisticated soup with the subtle flavour of dashi stock – a perfect starter for a dinner party. The quality of the soup relies on a well-flavoured dashi stock.

serves 4 as a starter

400g (14oz) spinach
800ml (1½ pints) dashi stock (see page 16)
½ tsp salt
about 1 tbsp light soy sauce
2 eggs, lightly beaten

Bring a large saucepan of water to the boil and blanch the spinach for 2–3 minutes, then immerse in a bowl of ice-cold water and drain well. Put the spinach on a sushi rolling mat, squeeze out any remaining water and roll into a thick cylinder. Cut the spinach roll into 4 equal pieces and set aside to keep warm.

Heat the dashi stock in a saucepan, not allowing it to boil, and adjusting the heat if necessary to keep it at a gentle simmer. Season the dashi with the salt and soy sauce to taste. Pour the beaten eggs through a slotted spoon into the stock, moving the spoon as you do so to create swirling strands. Bring the soup back to a gentle simmer and turn off the heat.

Place the spinach rolls in the middle of 4 warm soup dishes and gently ladle in the soup, trying not to disturb the spinach.

squid salad

This is a refreshing salad of squid blanched in rice vinegar and crunchy vegetables dressed with spicy mayonnaise. Ask your fishmonger to prepare the squid for you.

serves 4

400g (14oz) prepared squid
1 tbsp rice vinegar
1 red onion, thinly sliced
1 red pepper, deseeded and thinly sliced
1 yellow pepper, deseeded and thinly sliced
200g (7oz) mizuna or wild rocket leaves
1 tbsp cress, to garnish
4 tsp toasted white sesame seeds, to garnish
4 tsp toasted black sesame seeds, to garnish

for the salad dressing
4 tbsp good-quality mayonnaise
2 tbsp rice vinegar
1 tbsp light soy sauce
2 tbsp chilli sauce

Wash the inside of the squid body pouch with cold running water. Insert the blade of a small knife into the opening of the body and slit it open along one side. Score a criss-cross pattern on what was the inside with the tip of a knife, taking care not to cut too deeply. Cut into 5cm x 2.5cm (2in x 1in) pieces. Cut the tentacles into similar-size pieces.

Bring a saucepan of water to the boil and add the rice vinegar. Blanch the squid for 2–3 minutes, then briefly submerge it in a bowl of ice-cold water and drain. Mix all the ingredients for the dressing in a screwtop jar and shake well to combine.

Put the squid and all the prepared vegetables in a large salad bowl, pour the dressing over and toss together. Garnish with the cress and sesame seeds, and serve.

seaweed salad with crabmeat

This tangy salad is ideal as a starter or light meal. If you don't wish to cook and prepare your own crab, buy a ready-prepared crab from your local fishmonger.

serves 4

450g (1lb) crab, or 120g (4¼oz) cooked white
   crabmeat
25g (1oz) dried seaweed (see tip)
1 tsp crushed fresh root ginger
30ml (1fl oz) sanbaizu (see page 47)
4 tsp red pickled ginger (see tip), thinly sliced,
   to garnish

Place the crab in the freezer for 1 hour. Bring a large saucepan of water to the boil, drop in the crab and boil for 10–12 minutes. Drain and leave to cool.

Prepare the crab by twisting off the claws and legs. Crack these open and pull out any meat. Place the centre body on a chopping board and stand it up so that the shell is towards you. Force the body away from the shell using your thumbs or the heel of a knife. Pull away the gills from the sides of the central body and remove the white meat.

Soak the seaweed in a bowl of tepid water for 10–15 minutes – do not over-soak, as this will spoil the texture. Drain the softened seaweed and chill. Place the white crabmeat and 4 small, deep serving dishes in the refrigerator for 10–20 minutes.

Mix the grated ginger with the sanbaizu and refrigerate until just before serving.

When ready to serve, mix the seaweed and crabmeat in a bowl with the sanbaizu mixture and toss to dress. Arrange the seaweed and crabmeat mixture in small mounds in the chilled dishes. Top with the red pickled ginger and serve.

YO! Sushi tip

Do not add the sanbaizu mixture until just before serving so as not to discolour the salad and make it watery.

Use wakame or a bag of mixed seaweeds, which has several different varieties.

Red pickled ginger (beni shoga) is first pickled in salt and then red plum vinegar and red shiso leaves. It is sold in vacuum packs but can be difficult to get hold of; if you can't find it, use fresh root ginger instead.

tempura vegetables

Along with sushi and teriyaki, tempura is a universally recognised Japanese dish but it is often incorrectly perceived as being difficult to prepare. See pages 36–37 for step-by-step instructions for how to make light, crispy tempura every time.

serves 4

vegetable oil with 2 tbsp sesame oil, for deep-frying
1 small sweet potato, scrubbed clean and
   cut into 8 slices
1 small aubergine, cut into 8 slices
1 onion, cut horizontally into 4
4 fresh shiitake mushrooms, stems removed
1 red pepper, deseeded and cut into 4
1 green pepper, deseeded and cut into 4
200g (7oz) daikon (Japanese giant white radish),
   grated, to serve

for the dipping sauce
50ml (2fl oz) mirin
50ml (2fl oz) soy sauce
150ml (5fl oz) water
50ml (2fl oz) dried bonito flakes

for the batter
1 egg, lightly beaten
150ml (5fl oz) ice-cold water
100g (3$\frac{1}{2}$oz) fine plain flour, sifted

Start by making the dipping sauce. Put the mirin in a saucepan and bring to the boil for 2–3 minutes to burn off the alcohol, then add all the other ingredients. Reduce the heat and simmer for 3 minutes. Strain the sauce through a fine mesh sieve. Set it aside until you are ready to serve.

Have all the vegetables ready. Heat the oil to 170–180°C/325–350°F.

To make the batter, in a chilled mixing bowl, combine the beaten egg and the ice-cold water. Sift the flour into the bowl and mix quickly, making cutting motions with the handles of 2 wooden spoons.

Dip the sweet potato in the batter and drop into the oil, deep-fry for 3–4 minutes or until the batter turns opaque and crisp. Do not put in too much at a time (no more than three-quarters of the surface of the oil should be covered). With a pair of cooking chopsticks or tongs, turn the slices of sweet potato 2 or 3 times to cook evenly on both sides. Take them out and put them on a rack to drain, making sure not to pile them on top of one another as this will make the batter soggy. Cook all the other vegetables except the daikon and skim off any bits floating in the oil before you add each batch.

Arrange the cooked vegetables on 4 individual serving platters lined with rice paper. Put small mounds of daikon on the side and give each person some dipping sauce in a separate dish.

tempura prawns

Tempura, one of the most quintessentially Japanese dishes, has its origins in the West, as the Portuguese introduced it in the fifteenth century. Like so many foreign cooking styles and ingredients, tempura found its way into the Japanese kitchen and is now at the very centre of Japanese cuisine. This recipe is tempura at its simplest: light and crispy prawns served with nothing more than seasoned salt. See pages 36–37 for step-by-step instuctions.

serves 4

12 large, raw tiger prawns
vegetable oil with 2 tbsp sesame oil, for deep-frying
100g (3$\frac{1}{2}$oz) fine plain flour, sifted, for dusting
4 tbsp fine sea salt
$\frac{1}{2}$tsp matcha (green tea powder)

for the tempura batter
1 egg, lightly beaten
200ml (7fl oz) ice-cold water
100g (3$\frac{1}{2}$oz) fine plain flour, sifted

Pull off the heads of the prawns, remove the shells and discard. Make a shallow slit along the back of each prawn and remove the black vein. Turn the prawns on their backs and make 4 or 5 shallow cuts across their underside to stop them from curling up when cooked. Snip the tips of the tails and, with the blade of a knife, squeeze out any liquid.

Heat the oil in a cast-iron or heavy-based saucepan to 170–180°C/325–350°F. Mix the salt and matcha together and divide among 4 small dishes.

Now make the batter. Combine the egg and water in a chilled bowl, add the flour and mix briefly with the handles of 2 wooden spoons using cutting motions. Dust the prawns with the flour. Test the temperature of the oil by dropping in a drip of batter – it should sink to the middle before floating back up to the surface – and adjust the heat if necessary. Holding on to the tail of a prawn, dip it into the batter and quickly drop it in the oil. Deep-fry until crisp, turning it over 2–3 times using cooking chopsticks or tongs. Do not put too many prawns into the oil at a time, as this will lower the temperature and result in heavy, sticky batter.

Arrange the prawns on each plate and serve with the seasoned salt.

YO! Sushi tip
In Japan, the heads and shells are also dipped in tempura batter, deep-fried and eaten.

salmon curry tempura donburi

This recipes combines two of the most popular Japanese dishes – donburi and tempura. The crispy salmon tempura has a light curry flavour which goes wonderfully with the warm rice. See pages 36–37 for step-by-step instructions on making tempura.

serves 4

4 salmon fillets, each weighing 100g (3½oz)
vegetable oil, for deep-frying
4 tbsp fine plain flour, sifted
4 tbsp curry powder
800g (1lb 12oz) warm cooked rice (see pages 18–19)

for the sauce
75ml (3fl oz) mirin
250ml (9fl oz) water or dashi stock (see page 16)
75ml (3fl oz) soy sauce
2½ tbsp sugar
5g (⅛oz) bonito flakes

for the batter
2 eggs, lightly beaten
160ml (5¾fl oz) ice-cold water
175g (6oz) fine plain flour, sifted
4 tbsp curry powder

First make the sauce. Put the mirin in a saucepan and bring to the boil over a high heat, turn the heat down, add the rest of the sauce ingredients and simmer for 10 minutes. Strain the sauce through a sieve lined with kitchen paper or a coffee filter and keep warm.

Cut the salmon in fillets into bite-size pieces. Heat the oil to 170–180°C/325–350°F. Mix together the flour and curry powder and use to dust the salmon fillets. Make up the batter, dip in the salmon and deep-fry until crisp. Transfer to a rack to drain.

Divide the cooked rice between 4 warm serving bowls and pour over the sauce. Top each bowl with the salmon tempura and cover to steam for 2–3 minutes before serving.

YO! Sushi tip

This is a great recipe for using up leftover tempura. Heat the sauce to just below boiling point and put the tempura in for 30 seconds to reheat.

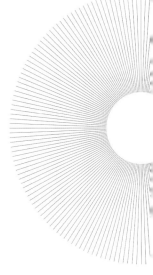

hairy prawns with rocket leaves

This is a spectacularly visual dish: succulent tiger prawns wrapped in kadaifi pastry and deep-fried to give them a crispy coating. Kadaifi pastry can be difficult to find sometimes, so this version calls for harusame noodles (*harusame* means 'spring rain') or fine vermicelli noodles to suit domestic kitchens. Harusame noodles are made from mung bean or potato starch. Transparent and very fine, they are less than 1mm (1/32in) thick, and puff up and turn white when deep-fried. Thai glass, vermicelli or cellophane noodles make excellent substitutes.

serves 4

12 raw tiger prawns
1 litre (1¾ pint) vegetable oil, for deep-frying
100g (3½oz) plain flour
2 eggs, lightly beaten, mixed with 2 tbsp water
100g (3½oz) dried harusame noodles, roughly
   chopped into 2.5cm (1in) lengths
200g (7oz) wild rocket leaves
1 lime, cut into 4 wedges

for the sauce
100ml (3½fl oz) mayonnaise
1 tbsp wasabi paste
1 tbsp rice vinegar
½ tbsp grated fresh root ginger

Pull the heads off the prawns and remove the shells and legs, leaving the tails intact. Make a shallow incision along the underside of the prawns to remove the black vein (see picture 1 on page 33).

Heat the oil in a heavy-based or cast-iron saucepan to 170-180°C/ 325-350°F (see page 37 for how to test the temperature). Dust the prawns with the flour, dip them in the egg and water mixture and then roll them in the harusame noodles, patting them between your hands to encourage the noodles to stick. Deep-fry the prawns until the noodles are crisp, cooking 3 or 4 prawns at a time and turning them 2 to 3 times. Take the cooked prawns out and put them on a paper-lined rack to drain off the excess oil.

Divide the rocket leaves among 4 plates and mix together all the ingredients for the sauce. Arrange 3 prawns per person on top of the rocket leaves, drizzle over the sauce when you are ready to eat and serve with the pieces of lime on the side.

baked scallops with spicy miso sauce

Baked in their shells on a bed of wakame seaweed and shiitake mushrooms, these luscious scallops are served with a chilli miso sauce. Ask your fishmonger to remove the scallops from their shells but to give you the shells with the scallops.

serves 4 as a starter

4 large fresh scallops with their shells
4 fresh shiitake mushrooms, stalks removed, thinly sliced
1 leek, trimmed and thinly cut
20g (¾oz) dried wakame seaweed, soaked in cold water for 10 minutes and drained
4 tbsp olive oil

for the spicy miso sauce
4 tbsp milk chocolate-coloured miso paste
1 tsp chilli sauce
1 tbsp sake

Preheat the oven to 190°C/375°F/gas mark 5. Scrub clean the outside of the deeper scallop shells and discard the top, flat shells. Clean the inside of the deeper shells and pat dry.

To make the sauce, combine the miso, chilli sauce and sake in a bowl. Add the scallops, mushrooms, leek and wakame and mix to coat them in the sauce. Ladle some of the spicy vegetable mixture onto each shell and place 1 scallop on top. Drizzle over the olive oil.

Bake the scallops in the oven for 8–10 minutes or until they are just cooked. Remove the scallops from the oven and serve.

YO! Sushi tip
If you can't get scallops with their shell, use ovenproof dishes, such as ramekins.

Try this recipe using oysters instead of scallops, but you will need only half as much of the wakame, shiitake and leek mixture and half the quantity of sauce.

new sashimi
with hot oil

This new way of serving sashimi, using hot oil, is very dramatic and is sure to impress your dinner guests.

serves 4

400g (14oz) sole fillet, skin removed
1 tsp garlic, crushed
1 large red chilli, deseeded and cut into rings
1 tbsp finely chopped chives
1 tbsp ponzu sauce (see page 47)
1 tbsp light soy sauce
2 tsp toasted white sesame seeds
100ml (3½fl oz) sunflower oil
1 tsp sesame oil

Cut the fish into wafer-thin slices (see page 24) and arrange them on a large serving plate. Dab some crushed garlic on top of each slice and place some chilli in the middle of each one. Sprinkle each piece of fish with chives and drizzle over the ponzu and soy sauce. Garnish with the sesame seeds. Put the plate in the refrigerator to chill for 10 minutes.

Mix the sunflower and sesame oils together in a small frying pan and heat until it is almost smoking. Take the fish out of the refrigerator and, just before serving, pour over the hot oil. Take great care not to burn yourself; stand slightly back from the plate as you pour, because the oil will spit and sizzle. Serve immediately.

YO! Sushi tip
Try this recipe with other white fish such as sea bream, sea bass or scallops.

beef sukiyaki

When Japan reopened to the rest of the world in the mid-nineteenth century under the rule of Emperor Meiji, a wave of change swept through the country. Every aspect of Japanese life was affected, including diet, and for the first time in a thousand years, Japanese people started eating meat, with beef sukiyaki becoming the most fashionable dish. Sukiyaki is normally cooked at the table on a portable stove with everyone welcome to join in.

serves 4

400g (14oz) beef sirloin, in 1 piece
2 onions, thinly sliced
2 leeks, trimmed and thinly cut
1 bunch fresh enoki mushrooms
1 block grilled tofu or deep-fried tofu, cut
    into 2.5cm (1in) cubes (see tip)
1 bunch watercress
400g (14oz) dried udon noodles
4 eggs

for the sauce
4 tbsp soy sauce
4 tbsp mirin
4 tbsp sake
3 tbsp sugar
200ml (7fl oz) dashi stock (see page 16)

About 30 minutes before you want to start cooking, trim the fat off the outside of the beef. Wrap it with cling film and place it in the freezer for 30 minutes (semi-freezing the beef makes it easier to slice). Meanwhile, combine all the ingredients for the sauce.

Slice the beef as thinly as possible. Put the onions and leek in a shallow frying pan and arrange the beef on top with the mushrooms, tofu and watercress. Pour in enough sauce to cover the underside of the beef and bring to the boil over a medium to high heat.

Meanwhile, cook the noodles in a separate saucepan, refresh with cold running water and drain (see page 22 for advice on cooking noodles). When the sauce begins to boil, crack the eggs into it to be poached alongside the beef. Reduce the heat and leave to simmer until the beef and eggs are cooked to your liking. Serve the beef and vegetables.

When all the beef and some of the vegetables have been eaten, reheat the noodles in the same pan and eat towards the end of the meal.

YO! Sushi tip
To cook the tofu, first drain it by wrapping in kitchen paper and leaving it to stand for 15 to 20 minutes. To grill or fry, brush the block with vegetable oil and grill under a hot grill, or fry over a high heat, for 5–8 minutes on both sides. Alternatively, deep-fry the block in vegetable oil until crisp and golden.

gunkan

Gunkan, or 'battleship', sushi is a variety of nigiri (hand-formed sushi) that is especially suitable for small or slippery toppings such as salmon roe, flying fish roe and sea urchin. Each recipe makes 8 gunkan. See pages 34–35 for step-by-step instructions.

ikura (salmon roe)

80g (3¼oz) ikura (salmon roe)
1 tbsp soy sauce
1 tbsp sake
80g (3¼oz) prepared sushi rice (see pages 19–21)
8 nori ribbons, 2.5cm (1in) wide
1 tbsp wasabi paste
2 tsp finely chopped chives

Have a bowl of cold water mixed with a little rice vinegar ready.

In a small bowl, mix the ikura with the soy sauce and sake, and set aside for the flavours to develop while you form the gunkan.

Moisten your hands with the vinegar solution to stop the rice sticking. With one hand take 3 teaspoons or 20g (¾oz) of the sushi rice (weigh it out until you gain more confidence) and shape it into a small ball. Press down with your thumb to make a slight depression, then transfer the rice to a clean chopping board. Wrap a piece of the nori ribbon around the rice and secure the end of the ribbon with a grain of rice.

With your index finger, smear a dab of wasabi where you made the depression. Spoon in 3 teaspoons of the ikura mixture and garnish with a sprinkling of finely chopped chives. Repeat the process 7 times more and serve 2 pieces per person.

tobiko

80g (3¼oz) prepared sushi rice (see pages 19–21)
8 nori ribbons, 2.5cm (1in) wide
1 tbsp wasabi paste
80g (3¼oz) tobiko (flying fish roe)

Make 8 pieces of gunkan sushi as described for ikura. Top with the tobiko.

crabmeat and wasabi mayonnaise

100g (3½oz) cooked white crabmeat
2 tbsp good-quality mayonnaise
80g (3¼oz) prepared sushi rice (see pages 19–21)
8 nori ribbons, 2.5cm (1in) wide
1 tbsp wasabi paste
2 tsp cress

In a small bowl, mix together the crabmeat and mayonnaise. Make 8 pieces of gunkan as for ikura gunkan on page 178. Top with the crabmeat mixture and garnish with a sprinkling of cress.

smoked salmon and spring onion

100g (3½oz) smoked salmon, chopped
2 spring onions, finely chopped
1 tbsp lime juice
1 tsp soy sauce
80g (3¼oz) prepared sushi rice (see pages 19–21)
8 nori ribbons, 2.5cm (1in) wide
1 tbsp wasabi paste

In a small bowl, mix together the smoked salmon, spring onions, lime juice and soy sauce. Make 8 pieces of gunkan as described for ikura gunkan (page 178). Top with the salmon mixture and serve.

crayfish and mango

80g (3¼oz) cooked shelled crayfish, drained and roughly chopped
40g (1½oz) ripe mango, finely chopped
2 tbsp finely chopped coriander leaves
1 tbsp lime juice
80g (3¼oz) prepared sushi rice (see pages 19–21)
8 nori ribbons, 2.5cm (1in) wide
1 tsp shichimi togarashi (Japanese seven-spice chilli powder)

In a small bowl mix together the crayfish, mango, coriander and lime juice. Make 8 pieces of gunkan as described for ikura gunkan (page 178), but without using wasabi. Top with the crayfish mixture, sprinkle with the shichimi togarashi and serve.

negitoro (tuna and spring onion)

100g (3½oz) tuna, finely chopped
4 spring onions, finely chopped
1 tbsp soy sauce
1 tsp shichimi togarashi (Japanese seven-spice chilli powder)
80g (3¼oz) prepared sushi rice (see pages 19–21)
8 nori ribbons, 2.5cm (1in) wide
1 tbsp wasabi paste

Mix together the tuna, spring onions, soy sauce and shichimi togarashi. Make 8 pieces of gunkan as described for ikura gunkan (page 178). Top with the tuna mixture and serve.

avocado and wasabi mayonnaise

100g (3½oz) ripe, Hass avocado, roughly chopped (about 1 avocado)
2 tbsp good-quality mayonnaise
1 tsp wasabi paste
1 tbsp toasted sesame seeds, coarsely ground
80g (3¼oz) prepared sushi rice (see pages 19–21)
8 nori ribbons, 2.5cm (1in) wide

Put the avocado in a small bowl, mash slightly with a fork and mix with the mayonnaise and wasabi paste. Add the sesame seeds and mix well. Make 8 pieces of gunkan as described for ikura gunkan (page 178), but without using the wasabi. Top with the avocado and wasabi mixture and serve.

green beans with gomadare

100g (3½oz) green beans, cut into 1cm (½in) lengths
80g (3¼oz) prepared sushi rice (see pages 19–21)
8 nori ribbons, 2.5cm (1in) wide

for the gomadare
4 tbsp toasted sesame seeds
½ tsp sugar
1 tbsp milk chocolate-coloured miso paste
1 tbsp mirin

Steam the beans for 2–3 minutes, refresh under cold running water and drain.

To make the gomadare, put the sesame seeds in a mortar and coarsely grind using a pestle. Add the sugar, miso and mirin and mix well. Mix the beans with the gomadare. Make 8 pieces of gunkan as described for ikura gunkan (page 178), but without using the wasabi. Top with the beans and serve.

daikon salad

Daikon (also called mooli) is a large white radish that came from China in the seventh century. Today it is one of the most widely grown vegetables in Japan. Known as a natural digestive, it is traditionally served as an accompaniment for sashimi and grilled fish.

200g (7oz) daikon, washed clean

Do not peel the daikon, as the skin is rich in vitamin C. Using a Japanese mandolin (or grater), grate it into a bowl of ice cold water. Place the shredded daikon in the refrigerator to refresh and crisp for 10–15 minutes, then drain well before serving.

YO! Sushi tip
Japanese mandolins are available from good kitchen shops or department stores and have inter-changeable blades. Do be careful though: mandolins have very sharp blades.

nigiri

Many people outside Japan think that *nigiri zushi,* or 'hand-formed' sushi, is the only kind of sushi. But in the fourteen hundred years that sushi has been evolving, nigiri is a comparative newcomer. *Nigiri zushi* is also known in Japan as *Edomae zushi* (meaning 'in front of Edo', Edo being the old name for Tokyo – in other words, Tokyo bay) reflecting its origins. Legend has it that in early nineteenth-century Edo an inventive sushi chef, Yohei Hanaya, came up with the idea of forming a rice ball in one hand and topping it with a slice of cooked or cured fish or shellfish from Tokyo bay, which once teemed with marine life.

Until the beginning of the twentieth century, at least, there were two distinct types of sushi shops: ordinary sushi shops that dealt mainly with takeaway and deliveries, and smaller, outdoor stands of the kind that used to be found on practically every street corner in Tokyo. These served mainly male customers in the evening, who ate standing up. After the end of the Second World War sushi stands began to disappear and sushi shops got bigger and started serving food indoors as women gradually began to eat outside the home. At the same time, nigiri shrank to bite-size pieces and the toppings, instead of being cooked or cured, tended to be raw.

Today, nigiri sushi is undisputedly the most popular kind of sushi both inside and outside Japan. Particularly within Japan, however, nigiri is considered best left to expert sushi chefs and is rarely made at home, on the grounds that there is more to the art of sushi making than just shaping the rice and putting a slice of raw fish on top. But that is no reason why the delights of nigiri should not be experienced in domestic kitchens. See pages 32–33 for step-by-step instructions. Each recipe makes 8 nigiri.

salmon

120g (4½oz) salmon fillet, skin removed
120g (4½oz) prepared sushi rice (see pages 19–21)
3 tsp wasabi paste

Cut the salmon into 8 equal slices, about 8mm
(⅓in) thick (see page 24).

Divide the prepared sushi rice into 8 equal
portions and make 8 nigiri pieces using the
method described on pages 32–33. Serve
2 per person.

prawn

3 tsp salt
8 raw, medium prawns
120g (4½oz) prepared sushi rice (see pages 19–21)
3 tsp wasabi paste
4 shiso leaves (optional)

Bring a saucepan of water to the boil and add
the salt. Thread each prawn along its length
onto a bamboo skewer. Cook the prawns in the
salted water for 1–2 minutes or until they begin
to turn bright orange, then take them out and
immediately plunge them into cold water to
stop them overcooking and to refresh their
colour. Drain, then remove the skewers by
gently turning the prawns. Cut off the heads
and remove the shells and legs. Insert a knife
into the underside to open them out, and use
the knife to take out the vein that runs down
their back (see picture on page 33).

Make 8 nigiri pieces as described on pages
32–33. Cut the shiso leaves down the centre to
make 8 half-moon shapes. Put half a shiso leaf
over the top of the prawn, tuck the ends
underneath the rice and serve.

tamago

120g (4½oz) Japanese rolled omelette (see page
   110)
120g (4½oz) prepared sushi rice (see pages 19–21)
2 tbsp cress
½ nori sheet

Cut the omelette into 8 slices, each one
1cm (½in) thick, 4cm (1½in) long and 2.5cm
(1in) wide.

Make 8 nigiri pieces as described on pages
32–33, topped with omelette. Cut the nori sheet
into 8 thin ribbons, 1cm (½in) wide and 10cm
(4in) long. Arrange the cress on top of the
omelette, place a nori ribbon across the top,
tucking both ends under the rice, and serve.

eel

In Japan, nearly half the annual
consumption of eels takes place on one
day in mid-summer – the Day of the Dog
– because Japanese people believe that
eating highly nutritious eels will get them
through the long, hot Japanese summer.
Outside Japan, ready-prepared grilled
eels coated in a sweet, soy-based sauce
are sold in vacuum packs.

120g (4½oz) ready-prepared eel
120g (4½oz) prepared sushi rice (see pages 19–21)
3 tsp wasabi paste
100g (3½oz) ripe avocado, sliced in thin wedges
   (about 1 avocado)
½ nori sheet, cut into 8 ribbons as above
1 tsp sansho pepper

Grilled eel that comes in a vacuum pack is best microwaved for 30 seconds on a medium heat to improve the texture. Take the eel out of the packet, halve it lengthways and cut it into 8 diamond-shaped pieces, roughly 5cm x 4cm (2in x 1½in).

Make 8 pieces of nigiri as described on pages 32–33. Put a piece of thinly sliced avocado on top of each piece of eel. Lay a nori ribbon across each nigiri, tucking both ends under the rice. Sprinkle with the sansho pepper and serve.

mackerel

120g (4½oz) mackerel fillet, marinated in sushi vinegar (see page 116)
120g (4½oz) prepared sushi rice (see pages 19–21)
3 tsp wasabi paste
1 tbsp grated fresh root ginger

Cut the marinated mackerel into 8 diamond-shape pieces, roughly 5cm x 4cm (2in x 1½in). Make 8 pieces of nigiri with the mackerel, as described on pages 32–33. Place a small pinch of the grated ginger on top and serve.

beetroot salmon

This is made with salmon that has been marinated with beetroot, the colours in this are stunning.

120g (4½oz) salmon fillet, sliced thinly as if for sashimi (see page 24)
10 slices raw beetroot, peeled and thinly sliced
100ml (3½fl oz) sushi vinegar
120g (4½oz) prepared sushi rice (see pages 19–21)
3 tsp wasabi paste

Put a slice of salmon in a shallow dish and cover with a layer of beetroot. Continue in this way until all the salmon and beetroot is used. Pour the sushi vinegar over the top. Leave to marinate for 15–20 minutes, then remove and drain the salmon, discarding the beetroot.

Make 8 nigiri pieces with the marinated salmon as described on pages 32–33 and serve.

sesame salmon

120g (4½oz) salmon fillet
2 tbsp fine plain flour, sifted
1 egg white, beaten until stiff
2 tbsp toasted black sesame seeds
1 tbsp vegetable oil
120g (4½oz) prepared sushi rice (see pages 19–21)
1 tbsp wasabi paste

Dust the salmon with the flour, coat with the egg white and sprinkle with the sesame seeds. Heat a non-stick frying pan over low heat, add the oil and cook the salmon for 2–3 minutes on each side.

Cut the salmon into 8 sashimi slices (see page 24). Makes 8 pieces of nigiri as described on pages 32–33 and serve.

chocolate inside-out roll with dipping sauce

This is so decadent. Why not indulge yourself!

makes 1 roll (8 pieces when cut)

for the ISO
½ nori sheet
200g (7oz) prepared sushi rice (see pages 19–21)
1 tbsp honey
1 tbsp hazelnuts, finely chopped
50g (2oz) mango, cut into strips
50g (2oz) melon, cut into strips
50g (2oz) strawberries, sliced into thin strips
100g (3½oz) plain chocolate, finely grated

for the chocolate sauce
200g (7oz) plain chocolate
50g (2oz) unsalted butter

Place the nori sheet on a chopping board and cover it with the prepared sushi rice. Turn it over and spread the honey over using the back of a spoon, then cover it with the hazelnuts, mango, melon and strawberries. Roll it up to make an ISO (see pages 30–31), then flip it over and roll it in the grated chocolate until it is coated.

Make the sauce by gently melting the plain chocolate and the butter in a saucepan over a very low heat.

Cut the roll into 8 pieces and drizzle with the chocolate sauce.

steamed pumpkin cake

This soft and squashy cake is perfect for any occasion, whether a special celebration or a casual family supper. You need a lot of mixing bowls for this recipe, but the finished cake is worth it.

serves 6

100g (3½oz) self-raising flour, sifted
75g (3oz) caster sugar
2 eggs, separated
2 tbsp unsalted butter, melted
30ml (1fl oz) coconut milk
200g (7oz) pumpkin, skinned, steamed and mashed
2 tbsp milk chocolate-coloured miso paste
2 tbsp mirin
1 tsp bicarbonate of soda
icing sugar, for dusting

Grease and line a 20.5cm (8in)-round cake tin with baking paper.

Take out a lidded saucepan large enough to hold the cake tin. Fill it half full with water and turn on the heat so that the water is boiling by the time you are ready to cook the cake. Have to hand a heat-proof saucer or plate that will sit in the bottom of the saucepan and serve as a trivet on which to stand the cake tin.

Sift the flour and the sugar together into a large mixing bowl. In a separate bowl, beat the egg whites until they form soft peaks. In a third large bowl beat the egg yolks, the melted butter and coconut milk until the mixture is pale and creamy. Fold in the egg white and add the flour and sugar mixture, using cut-and-fold motions.

Take another large bowl and mix the pumpkin, miso, mirin and bicarbonate of soda until fluffy. Combine the contents of the 2 bowls using cut-and-fold motions to keep the air bubbles intact so that the final mixture is light.

Put the mixture in the cake tin and set the tin in the saucepan, adjusting the level of the water so that the cake tin is above the water level. Cover the pan and leave to steam for 30–45 minutes or until the cake has risen in a dome shape. Top up with boiling water if necessary. Remove the cake from the saucepan and leave to cool in the tin. Turn the cake out of the tin and set aside to cool a little more before dusting with the icing sugar and serving.

resources

useful addresses

Japanese ingredients and equipment can be found in larger supermarkets, specialist stores and ordered online.

Japan Centre
212 Piccadilly
London W1J 9HX
0870 162 0255
www.japancentre.com

Arigato
48-50 Brewer Street
London W1F 9TG
020 7287 1722

Atari-ya Foods – Finchley
595 High Road
North Finchley
London N12 0DY
020 8446 6669

Atari-ya Foods – Golders Green
15-16 Monkville Parade
Finchley Road
London NW11 0AL
020 8458 7626

Atari-ya Foods – Kingston
44 Coombe Road
Kingston-upon-Thames
Surrey KT2 7AF
020 8547 9891

Atrai-ya Foods – Oriental City
399 Edgware Road
London
NW9 0JJ
020 8205 0091
www.atariya.co.uk/en/index.html

websites

www.okinami.com
www.tazakigroup.com
www.mountfuji.co.uk
www.clearspring.co.uk
www.japanesekitchen.co.uk
www.ocado.com

To find your local YO! Sushi restaurant, read about the latest offers and menus or order YO! To Go, see www.yosushi.com.

YO! Sushi
95 Farringdon Road
London
EC1R 3BT
020 7841 0700

index

Page numbers in **bold** denote a photograph

acknowledgements

Creating a book is like embarking on a long journey: unexpected difficulties, unplanned events and surprising outcomes, but what makes the experience unforgettable and life enriching is the people that are met along the way. It is my privilege as an author to thank them at the journey's end.

My first and big thanks go to two highly inspiring men: Robin Rowland, the CEO of YO! Sushi for the inspiration to create a YO! Sushi cookbook, and my agent, Ivan Mulcahy, for his tireless steady stewardship and personal encouragement throughout the project. Without these men, this book would not have happened.

Thank you to Georgia Hall and Maya Hart at YO! Sushi for their wonderful support and help.

My special thanks to everyone at Collins, but especially to Jenny Heller, the Editorial Director for her vision and trust, and the professional but very warm support she gave me. Enormous thanks to the gentle and calm Lizzy Gray, for her hard work in making the book a reality. It has been my fortune and pleasure to work with a team of such talented people, including Emma Ewbank and Nicky Barneby who designed the book.

I must extend my thanks to Jane Suthering, the food stylist, for recreating my recipes beautifully and to the photographer, Frank Adam for taking such gorgeous photos.

Last but not least, I would like to thank my husband, Stephen, for his endless unpaid support for my work and Maxi, Frederick and Dominic, our three boys, for being unofficial but reliable guinea pigs and for patiently putting up with me. I am so lucky to have you and without you all, none of this is worthwhile.

picture acknowledgements

The publishers and YO! Sushi would like to thank the following photographers for their images: Dave Flindall, dave@delarge.co.uk (pp6, 43, 48, 61, 65, 67, 79, 104, 113, 118-119, and inside cover); Gareth Gardner, gareth@garethgardner.demon.co.uk (p56); Adam Lawrence, adam@adamlawrence.com (pp48, 67, 147, 157, 172); Graham Young, graham@grahamyoung.com (p2 and inside cover); Simon Brooke-Webb, simon@sbw-photo.com (p7).